GOD LIVES—IN THE SUBURBS

GOD LIVES—
IN THE SUBURBS

by John V. Chervokas

Doubleday
New York
1987

Library of Congress Cataloging in Publication Data
Chervokas, John, 1936–
    God lives—in the suburbs.

    1. Christian life—Anecdotes, facetiae, satire, etc.
2. Suburbs—United States.   I. Title.
BV4517.C48   1987   248   87-8853
ISBN 0-385-23928-9

For Jason, Joshua and Jessica—
with a j, as in joy

CONTENTS

Forelogue   ix

GOD LIVES—IN THE SUBURBS   1

SUNDAY NIGHT—*Raising Funds, Raising Eyebrows,
Raising the Roof*   3

MONDAY MORNING—*Bending, Boiling and Belittling*   10

MONDAY AFTERNOON—*When the "Gee, They
Don't Look Like Saints" Come Marching In*   14

MONDAY NIGHT—*The Village Board and "I'm Bored"*   17

TUESDAY MORNING—*Loving Lists and Noodging Notes*   24

TUESDAY AFTERNOON—*What's Your Handicap? God.*   29

TUESDAY NIGHT—*Here's Grandma, There's Alex, Where's
Inky?*   34

WEDNESDAY MORNING—*Carless in Camelot*   40

WEDNESDAY AFTERNOON—*Meditating Among the
Marigolds, Reflecting on the Roof*   45

WEDNESDAY NIGHT—*Frzzbk, Blang, Brring, Skritch
Skritch, Hrgh Hrgh*   52

THURSDAY MORNING—*Permanent Relationships*   57

THURSDAY AFTERNOON—*Chipped off the Old Block*   61

THURSDAY NIGHT—*TV Prayers*   67

FRIDAY MORNING—*"Guess Who I Ran into at the
Bank Today, Honey?"*   86

viii CONTENTS

FRIDAY AFTERNOON—*Realty vs. Reality* 91

FRIDAY NIGHT—*An Early Movie and a Late, Late Night* 96

SUBURBAN RITES 108

SATURDAY MORNING—*Taking God to Task . . .
After Task . . . After Task* 110

SATURDAY AFTERNOON—*Running in the Family.
Catching in the Family. Sliding, Jumping and Diving
in the Family* 123

SATURDAY NIGHT—*The Charity—But Just How Much
Charity?—Ball* 130

SUNDAY MORNING—*The Definite Article* 139

SUNDAY AFTERNOON—*Kicks* 148

FORELOGUE

Should you prefer to read the forelogue *after* the main text, as an epiword, feel free to do so. Forelogues and epiwords are interchangeable.

My point is that after reading the final draft of the manuscript it struck me how many characters, however cameotically, appear in this book. Dozens upon dozens of suburbanites play a role, say a word, make their presence known.

This is important to note now—and remember later, because, in our suburban lives, each of us impinges on, responds to, influences and is influenced by scores of other suburban lives each day. Our shared humanity is both our arena and our strength.

I hope I have given you a true picture of the arena.

I trust we will continue to give each other strength.

GOD LIVES—IN THE SUBURBS

GOD LIVES—
IN THE SUBURBS

This is not a challenge to city dwellers and urban theologians. I am not claiming a geographic or a life-style exclusivity for God. Should you maintain that God lives in a tenement, a hotel room, a pied-à-terre or a penthouse co-op you won't get any argument from me. It's just that God happens to be in the suburbs so much, day after day, hour after hour—at patio cookouts, at pool parties, at Garden Club meetings, on the tennis court, at the post office, at the Village Board meetings, at back-to-school nights, at volunteer firemen's parades—that's it's rather obvious He has roots there.

Maybe I should emend that. Obvious? Just *how* obvious? Is God's presence in the suburbs all that obvious? In fact, is God's presence in the suburbs all that important—or even needed? Why should God, after all, choose to invest His timelessness in a place where people are well off, where life is consummately kapokally comfortable, where lawns are, more or less, green? Shouldn't God be more concerned, primarily concerned, with the poor, the homeless, the troubled, the forlorn?

Whoa! Let me stop myself—and maybe stop you, too. I don't intend to get into a brouhaha over where most of God's efforts—and therefore *our* efforts—ought to be directed. Don't think that there's a social-consciousness-raising treatise just ahead. No. Not at all. My sole and simple suggestion is that, from a few delightful decades of observation, it seems to me that God is a very involved, very active suburbanite—and isn't it lucky for us that He is?

What follows is, then, a sharing of those observations. In that sharing you might realize that God was at your last cocktail party or at yesterday's bridge tournament at The Club. He was there all the time and you didn't notice. Not that you were intentionally snubbing God. No, you just didn't know *how* to notice Him. Your attention was centered on—and understandably so—the lukewarm pigs-in-the-blanket ("Couldn't they have afforded some fancier hors d'oeuvres, stuffed mushrooms at the very least?") or the fact that your partner should have led with her spades, not her diamonds ("How long has she been playing bridge?"). It's more than likely that you didn't notice God because of the distractions, programmed and almost inescapable distractions, that crop up every single suburban day. With all these distractions vying for your attention (screaming for and insisting upon your attention), God just didn't seem as relevant, as fitting, as necessary as He does in other situations.

But then again, is there really *any* situation in which God, if we so wished, couldn't be, wouldn't be relevant? Look at it this way: if God has made a commitment to the suburbs, *our* suburbs, shouldn't we notice that commitment, applaud it and respond to it in some fashion?

We borrow tools from our suburban neighbors. We borrow money from our suburban banker. We depend on our suburban friends for consolation and cocktails. We rely on our suburban service people for warmth, protection and mail. Well, then, what about our fellow suburbanite God? Can't we have the same sort of relationship with God that we have with all those people who happen to share our zip code?

Of course we can.

If we so choose.

And there are so many opportunities that we might choose to choose. Throughout the week there are dozens, maybe even hundreds, of suburban situations in which we might want to include God, if not as a focal figure, certainly as one of the group huddled by the fireplace (real logs, please, no phony ones on gas jets) or one of the gang at The Nineteenth Hole (although you might not choose to include Him in when you roll for the drinks). This book is about how we in our "beloved burbs" might include God in our week. Like the week just ahead.

SUNDAY NIGHT

*Raising Funds, Raising Eyebrows,
Raising the Roof*

After seven on a Sunday night the various members of a suburban family can very often be found girding their loins (Calvin Klein-covered loins, some of them) for the Monday morning a few hours away. She is getting her aerobic gear (tights, shorts, leg warmers, workout mat) together. He is getting his commuting gear (attaché case, calculator, latest Robert Ludlum novel) together. They are amassing their school gear (frayed notebooks, baseball glove, Madonna tape, birthday present for Margie) in a heap in the center of their respective bedrooms.

This gathering ritual is interrupted by the ringing of the phone, the ring coming from any and all of the three extensions. The familial extensions, the kids, race to the phone. The winner of the race snatches the nearest phone and disappointedly shouts, "Oh, Mom. Or Dad. It's for one of . . . either of . . . you."

The children feel disappointed when *any* call isn't for one of them. And with this call, no matter which parent takes it, there is adult disappointment as well. Disappointment and a wince. Not a subtle wince either. A broad, pained wince. That's because the voice on the other end of the line says, "Good evening. Hope I didn't catch you at a bad time. I'm Irma Maxwell calling on behalf of the Village Ambulance Corps. As you might have heard or read, we are launching a drive to raise a hundred thousand dollars to buy some much needed new emergency equipment, and . . ."

And?

And, oooo, are you bugged!

A fund-raising call, another fund-raising call.

You wince.

You roll your eyes.

And what do you do?

You lie.

But such a little lie, such an innocuous untruth. "Oh, I'm sorry, yes . . . fine cause . . . but you *did* catch us at a bad time . . . we're right in the middle of dinner . . . you might call at some other time . . . yes, some other time . . . thanks . . . 'bye."

Now, who's been hurt by this expedient fib? Certainly not the fibber. And not the telephone solicitor, either. Nor, really, has the Village Ambulance Corps suffered. You'll make a modest contribution to the drive in due time. So no one has been hurt by the little white lie. But no one has been cheered, either.

Cheered?

Cheered.

One obligation of this humanity of ours that we share with billions of souls past, and potentially skillions of souls to come, is the obligation to cheer one another on, to keep slapping each other figuratively, if not literally, on the rump as we lope through this temporal part of life.

Our cheering needn't be loud or overly physical. Loud cheering and overly physical rooting can be read, in this context, as phony. We can't go high-fiving our way through life, no matter how much Sunday-after-noon football would lead us to believe we can. Ah, but we *can* cheer one another on in little gentle ways. We can cheer one another on with gentle cheering language, language like: "I must say, Irma, you're a very brave person to be doing this. I could never ask someone for money, especially over the phone. We're rather busy here at home right now, but the two of us will talk it over and we're familiar with all the good you do and certainly we'll make a contribution. And listen—good luck with the drive. Hope you go over the top. In fact, I'll say a prayer that you do."

There's a stunned silence on the other end of the phone. A prayer? Irma, just one of the eighty-nine million Americans who give up their time to work as volunteers, can't believe that this person is going to say a prayer for the drive, for the effort, and for Irma's role in it. Is the person offering the prayer silly . . . or sanctimonious?

Neither. Neither silly *nor* sanctimonious. Rather, the person is being *sensitive.*

Praying isn't a sign of sanctimony. Sanctimony, I'm afraid, can be an awfully pejorative word. In fact, praying isn't necessarily a sign of sanctity, either. It *can* be, but it doesn't have to be. Yet praying *is* almost always a sign of sensitivity, sensitivity for the human condition, sensitivity to the fact that Someone created the human condition and is in a position to comfort the human condition.

As you coil your way back to the kitchen (where most adult calls are received) to hang up the phone (with the extra-long extension cord that permits far-ranging pacing) you might say to God, not Irma, but to God *about* Irma:

> Blessed the goodness and gumption
> Of all those, dear God,
> Who ask for money
> For things that matter so much
> In the way lives are lived
> And improved,
> And, sometimes, saved.
> Be solicitous, Father,
> Of all those solicitors
> Who swallow their pride
> And shelve their ego
> In order to ask us
> To be the giving creatures
> You meant us to be.
> Amen.

The problem mentioned in that quickie chat with the Creator, the problem of self in conflict with selflessness, brings us quite naturally, if not all that pleasantly, to raising eyebrows. Whose eyebrows? Not *our* eyebrows, but the eyebrows of those around us, the eyebrows of all those whom we perceive to be in a position to make value judgments on us, on us and our very being.

Does God make the snap judgments we sense people make on us? What about that? Have Divine Eyebrows ever been raised at anything? A thought. Just a thought.

At any rate, if not God's, certainly the eyebrows of God's earth-fixed images have been raised a few millimeters when a daughter—or even son nowadays—proclaims, "I'm going upstairs to put a green streak in my hair."

Green streak? Aaarggghh!

Why?

Why?

To be different?

Or *not* to be different?

To stand out at tonight's party?

Or to blend in at tonight's party with all the other kids of equally ghastly, wildly streaked hair?

Our child knows, or senses, that people will judge both the hair and the person beneath it to be: dopey,

nerdy

or

moofy

if the coif is not "with it." Eyebrows, you see, will be raised in some dimension of scorn (as they surely will by the child's parents, but for another reason) for not taking a punky and/or funky (*p*'s and *f*'s are so interchangeable nowadays) attitude by spraying the hair.

We will cringe when a son or daughter decides to tinge those precious locks, yet haven't some of us been heard to say to wife and kids, "I wonder what the reaction would be at the office if I grew a beard over vacation"?

It's not that he needs a beard. He's not yearning for a growth to protect himself against the winter wind or to mask his less-than-lantern jaw. No, it's "I wonder what the reaction would be at the office . . ." that's the motivation to leave Trac II in the medicine chest for a couple of weeks.

Well, then, does he feel he's not getting the recognition he deserves for his work, his wit, his taste in ties? Why does he crave this extra attention? Does he feel he's developing into a corporate cipher, so in order to make his presence *re*-known he'll try some kind of radical facial change? Worse yet, what if he comes back to the office two Mondays hence, gloriously bristly—*and no one notices?*

Why does he, why do almost all of us, especially in the suburbs, *want* to raise eyebrows?

Clearly we need corroboration and approbation. We need some sort of okay from anyplace and everyplace that we are, indeed, one-of-a-kind human beings. And if it takes something as buckeyed as growing a full beard to pull it off, we're willing to do it.

And we're willing to use any of the thousands of means our fertile imagination can readily come up with. This need to elevate eyebrows need not require us to do something very dramatic or outlandish to our person. We can alter our image as well as our body, thereby allegedly gaining the grudging attention of our suburban peers. Besides hitting the old green aerosol spray can or tucking away the Gillette razor, we might choose to consider something like:

"Let's get a Jaguar."

Now, that's the sort of move we believe will not only raise the eyebrows of our peers a noticeable notch or two, but it will set their chins sagging, dropping them smack into their white-wine spritzers.

"Have you heard? Phil and Janice just got a Jag . . . a dark blue Jaguar?" Peer One will say.

"Whose idea was it?" wonders Peer Two.

And from Peer Three comes the answer, "I think Janice's."

"No," Peer One argues, "she's not that showy. It was probably Phil's idea."

Peer Three defends her guess. "Janice has been acting different lately. She's changing. I've noticed."

NOTICED! People *are* noticing. That's the whole point. That's why we're doing it in the first place. We rage to be seen, and be seen in a special way, a unique way, because *we* are snowflakes, *we* are fingerprints, *we* are one-of-a-kind.

Yet . . .

Yet back at the raised split-level manse on a Sunday night you can imagine the scene when all these potential eyebrow raisers announce their particular raising d'êtres at approximately the same time. There's enough tension in the house, with people thinking about tomorrow and planning for tomorrow, without the attention-getting declarations that follow:

"I'm going upstairs to put a green streak in my hair," says Jennifer, age sixteen.

"I wonder what the reaction would be at the office if I grew a beard over vacation," says Phil, forty-four.

"Let's get a Jaguar," says Janice, forty-two.

And the roof of the raised ranch is raised by another foot or so. Although the three can be said to love one another and wish the best for one another, being noticed or not being noticed, being one of the crowd or standing out in the crowd, making a statement consistent with either one's own feelings or the feelings of the prevailing Status Pacesetters, is "for me only." For me—and not for thee.

For example, when Jennifer suggests green hair and Janice suggests a Jaguar, Phil thinks it's ostentatious, pretentious, asinine and some other things not quite that polysyllabic. On the other hand, Phil not shaving for fourteen days, as Phil sees it, is one smart cosmetic move. That's all. Nothing more than that. Just a smart and stylish and totally appropriate cosmetic move.

And so Jennifer, sixteen, Phil, forty-four, and Janice, forty-two, will holler at each other and at no one in particular long into the Sunday night. Each will quarrel with the other's motivations and the various avenues that the family members have chosen to say something "of substance" about themselves.

That's part of the rub. And an increasingly more expensive rub at that. We all choose substances to supposedly say something "of substance" about ourselves. We look for tangibles (and visibles and audibles and smellables) to set us apart. We choose green dye and facial hair and forty thousand dollars' worth of sheet metal to say, "Look at me . . . look at me . . . don't you just love me?"

Okay, if not "love me," then you certainly must either admire me or respect me or think me one of God's favorite creations. Why "favorite"? Because I have the God-given confidence to dye my hair, the God-given self-assuredness to grow a beard, the God-given wherewithal to afford a Jaguar. Now, all of that is human, isn't it? All of that is part of our makeup as mortals, isn't it? Oh yes, it's human all right. Human, yes; pretty, no.

Imagine if all of us—Jennifer and Janice and Phil (and B.J. and Phil, Jr., the other family members, who aren't any less human than Mom and Dad and Sis)—were able to stop in mid-ego declaration and realize that we are *already* one-of-a-kind. Each one of us has been created as something unique, made that way long before we decided to remake ourselves into some flamboyant something or other.

Come to think of it, remaking ourselves is a rather arrogant act. Embellishing, improving, touching up the rough edges is fine, but remaking ourselves for the sake of being supposedly deemed special is saying to God, "You didn't do it quite right. Listen, God, I've got a better idea on how I should be. Let me show You. Let me fix myself up."

Now, in the midst of the family shouting and finger-waving, some of it sitcom ludicrous, in the midst of all this silliness precipitated by the imagined need to *look* different, one expression is shouted more than any other. Usually the expression is contagious: once one person uses it, so does another familial roof raiser. And that phrase is, *What are you trying to prove?*

"Growing a beard at your age! What in the world are you trying to prove, Phil?"

"What are *you* trying to prove, Janice? That we can really *afford* a Jaguar?"

The next time you hear yourself shouting out that question, or hear it yipped at you, yip it right back, but not at the person challenging you, but to your fellow suburbanite God. Yes, you might like to pause in your confrontation and say something like this to God:

What are *You* trying to prove, God,
By being so generous to me
And to all those around me?
That we aren't able to cope with Your generosity?
That we want even more rewards,
More respect, more recognition
As being super-special people?

What are You trying to prove, God,
Other than the frightening fact
That we are uncomfortable with our lot,
No matter how lovely that lot really is?

If that's so, or rather, because that's so,
Dear God, help us to change.
Help us strengthen our relationships
With each other—
And with You,
So that we don't find ourselves
Snarling, bickering and snapping
Over trappings
Of success
That really aren't.
Amen.

MONDAY MORNING

Bending, Boiling and Belittling

Did the great contemplatives ever sweat while meditating? Whether that's a question worth meditating on is probably not worth meditating on. No matter. Now you, Janice, are contorting your body into positions you never considered to be even fetally possible. You stand and you jump, you bounce and you flounce to the latest Tina Turner song. You pantingly appreciate the fact that, in this half-hour daily frenzy, you're doing your lungs and heart a big favor.

Aerobics in the A.M., or any ad-lib early-morning exercise, for that matter, gives a body a vigorous impetus to embrace the day. Wouldn't it be wonderful to be able to go through the entire day with the enthusiasm and arm-flailing animation we exhibit during morning exercise? Of course there are lists in your head of the tasks trivial and significant— and how do you tell them apart?—of your day. But, as your shocking purple sweat suit begins to show damp signs of aerobic stress, you might want to mention the day ahead to God. Even Tina's screech-song can't drown out your silent but nonetheless rhythmical, mute but melodic, good morning to God:

> I'm toning and tightening this body, God,
> So I can enjoy Your gift, this life,
> As long as I can.
> As for that *snippet* of life

That we call "today,"
Huffing, I wish,
And puffing, I pray,
For the strength to be
All you expect me to be,
Plus a day that's
More or less
Hassle free.
Amen.

Unlike Janice, her husband hasn't had a chance to ask God for a hassle-free day yet. That's because Phil is already being hassled. His equilibrium, his Type-A-ness is so rattled, Phil can't even ponder the weightier morning questions facing him, such as whether to opt for the sesame bagel or the pumpernickel one. Given the state he's in, how could Phil ever be expected to think of a good morning to God?

And just what is causing all this trouble for Phil?

A full train.

When the 6:33 pulls into his station, there's not a single empty seat to be seen. Every last one has been taken at stations up the line. No seats. But plenty of heat. The heat is on full blast. The conductor can't seem to turn it off.

So Phil's first excursion out of his suburban oasis this week is one of frustration—teeth-grinding, sweat-wiping, under-one's-breath-griping frustration.

Frustration is an effete word. It's also an effete attitude. Frustration implies impotency, an inability to deal with an unpleasant situation.

The word, considering its colorful heritage, deserves a better linguistic fate—and a better definition. Frustration comes from the Latin *frustrare* which means "to deceive" or "to trick." The way the word is used today does not necessarily mean that to have been frustrated you have been deceived or tricked. Rather, it means you have been neglected or overlooked or discomforted in some fashion.

Frustration, which comes from neglect or discomfort, considering all the much more serious woes plaguing humanity, is, then, a rather second-rate emotion. In fact, it's hardly worth the effort to experience such an emotion. Why should we bother suffering frustration? Can't we somehow fight it? Avoid it? Refuse to succumb to it? But how? How about this way?

I hope, God, You, who can do everything,
Appreciate me this minute,
Me, who can do absolutely nothing
About the heat,
The lack of seat,
The fact that I'll be on my feet
For nearly an hour.
Since it's in Your power,
Father, turn these first few
Pangs of frustration
Into blessed resignation,
A time for me to pause and pray
For people who could use some heat,
For people who aren't able to stand,
For people for whom frustration
Has become a way of life.
Amen.

As for B.J., his morning transportation isn't uncomfortable the way his father's is. B.J.'s school bus isn't hot. B.J. also has a seat. Actually he *has* to have a seat, according to safety regulations.

Yes, B.J.'s ride to school is quite comfortable. For B.J.

For B.J.'s companions, however, the ride may not be all that pleasant. That's because of B.J.'s sharp twelve-year-old wit and even sharper twelve-year-old tongue.

B.J., like so many youngsters, has polished his wit by watching a great deal of television—and watching his parents. On television he has seen stand-up comics and sitcom series whose humor is drawn from new and inventive ways of belittling people. The same holds true for so many commercials. Television commercials often derive "it caught my eye" interest from poking fun at people's foibles. Some go so far as to accentuate people's physical idiosyncrasies.

As for learning the art of zinging from Mom and Dad, B.J. is an observant scion indeed. He's heard Dad talk of his client as being "a legend in his own mind." He's heard Mom talk about Aunt Harriet's new "Phyllis Diller hair-do." So when B.J. sees a girl with braces on, he asks her if she attracts lightning. And when B.J. sits on the bus next to a boy all dressed up for his class picture, B.J. starts kidding him about his "fruit suit."

B.J. thinks he's being clever. After all, aren't Richard Pryor and Joan Rivers and Dad clever?

If B.J., Dad and Mom are all that clever, one of them, sooner or later, will hit upon this supposition and pass the thought along to the other family members (and maybe even to Richard Pryor and Joan Rivers): belittling a person is another way of saying to God that He screwed up.

How so? Well, when we criticize a product, for whatever reason, we are actually criticizing the maker of that product, aren't we? The same holds true when we knock an individual. We are really saying that, in the knockee's case, God the Creator apparently didn't give it His best shot.

Are any of us comfortable with that thought?

MONDAY AFTERNOON

When the "Gee, They Don't Look Like Saints" Come Marching In

Had you first met them at a PTA meeting or bumped into them at a political rally, you most surely would have been as civil and courteous as you could possibly be. But when they arrive at your home in the guise of tradespeople, your demeanor, and especially your language, switch, in an almost instinctive and instantaneous fashion, into that uppity idiom known by a linguist or two as Hirer Haughty.

No longer are you and they equals, as you would have been at the PTA meeting, chatting about the pros and cons of the new humanities curriculum. Neither are you and that tradesperson equal taxpayers commiserating as you might have done at the political meeting about the Southside zoning issue and the chances of a mini shopping center springing up. No. You (capital Y) are now the homeowner, and this man (itty-bitty m) in denim and scuffed workboots and wrinkled baseball cap is a . . . is a . . . tree pruner. At least that's the way things are from your employer point of view.

Hirer Haughty, as spoken in any language, is a harsh, abrasive form of speech. It sounds especially awful in English. It sounds even worse when spoken by a suburbanite.

Hirer Haughty, strangely enough, is rare in the city. That's because a city dweller doesn't often run across one of his service people in a social situation. In suburbia, however, there are any number of times when you can exchange views other than horticultural with your tree pruner under a socially neutral tree. At the PTA meeting, for example.

Why, then, must we lapse into Hirer Haughty when the man at the door with whom we shared some intelligent opinions and altogether pleasant words (many of them polysyllabic) reveals himself to be a tradesman, albeit a specially skilled individual who has come to perform a service for us?

Why, for instance, do we say to the plumber as we leave him to his ratchets and wrenches, "And be sure the kitchen is clean when you finish"?

Why do we say to the piano tuner, "What do you mean, 'the piano is fine'? My daughter says that the B sharp is way off"?

And why do we snap back at the piano tuner, "I know . . . I know . . ." when he tells us there *is* no B sharp?

Why?

Because we believe that if we are paying for a service we are somehow above the person performing that service. This arrogance applies, in a strange but significant way, only to services performed in and around our home.

Have you noticed? The same person who will chew out the painter for not mixing up exactly the right shade of peach ("It's too ripe, I want it not quite ripe") will shrink when the captain in a fancy restaurant tells him he should never have ordered that excellent St. Émilion when eating artichoke vinaigrette.

The householder who will bark orders to the gardener as he digs up a patch of hostas ("Careful, or you'll hack up all the corms") will be the same householder who will sit in semi-awe of his barber when the barber suggests a radical razor cut this time around.

I've concluded that the difference in our attitude has to do with ownership. If we own the house, or property or car, and you, painter, gardener, or mechanic, are paid to work on our house or property or car, we can speak to you in Hirer Haughty and not feel a single twinge of guilt.

If, on the other hand, we retain, however temporarily, certain specialists to deal in areas that we don't "own"—e.g., restaurants, dress shops, banks—we will readily and happily yield to the expertise of maître d's, dressmakers and bankers.

When the tree pruner pays a visit to Janice and Phil, Janice and Phil will make sure the pruner gets the tall hemlock hedge in the back trimmed properly, no matter how loud and snippily explicit their direc-tives have to be. After all, Barney, the tree pruner, is getting $690 for the job—that's the way Phil rationalizes his haughtiness. Barney ex-pects to be dictated to—that's Janice's rationalization.

Yes, but what if we assumed this: that Barney, for his life moment cast as a tree pruner, a.k.a. landscape specialist, is in actuality a *saint in training.* What if we looked at Barney and the cleaning woman and the newsboy and the roofer and the electrician and the chimney sweep as doing whatever they can do in their *life* roles, all the while having their hopes focused on what their *after*life roles will be? What if our fellow suburbanite and neighbor God put the bug into our head and soul that all of us are potential saints, whether we own the hemlock hedge or are commissioned to trim it? What might happen to us if we considered every single passing Barney in our life to be made not just of the *right* stuff, but of *holy* stuff? What?

W. H. Auden gives us a hint. He wrote, "I have met in my life two persons, one a man and the other a woman, who convinced me that they were persons of sanctity. Utterly different in character, upbringing and interests as they were, their effect on me was the same. In their presence I felt myself to be ten times as nice, ten times as intelligent, ten times as good-looking as I really am."

In a slightly perverse/reverse way, Barney almost does for Janice and Phil what Auden's two persons did for him. Janice, pridefully I'm afraid, probably considers herself quite a bit more intelligent than Bar-ney the tree pruner. Phil, eying the scraggly hair sticking out from under Barney's baseball cap, probably considers himself to be better-looking than the hired hand. But do either Janice or Phil, yakking away at Barney, giving him crisp and curt instructions, find themselves to be any *nicer* than the man up in the hemlocks? Hardly. At least not if they are honest enough with themselves.

If we could really believe that in a particular person's presence we felt nicer, more intelligent and better-looking, wouldn't we be much more likely to notice and respond to the possible sanctity of that per-son? Not in comparing ourselves with that person, as Janice and Phil, consciously or unconsciously, have done. But in the absolute.

Take a look at that beat-up truck in front of the house. What does it say on the door? "Barney's Lawn and Garden Care—Tree Pruning"? Look again. Oh, yeah. "*Saint* Barney's Lawn and Garden Care—Tree Pruning."

MONDAY NIGHT

The Village Board and "I'm Bored"

God hasn't missed a village board meeting since the community was founded, back in 17-whatever. With candidates for the board always talking about "commitment" and an 80 percent attendance record at board meetings being proof of same, God's 100 percent attendance record would make him a shoo-in for a seat. But God's not a candidate. Janice is.

(An explanation, perhaps a few pages late, on why I am referring to God as male. Quite simply, because I am male. I appreciate and respect the fact that, for some women, God is a woman. I have no quarrel with that. I *do* have a quarrel, however, with having to write He/She or She/He every time a divine pronoun is called for. So please, for the sake of simplicity of prose, if for no other reason, accept my male God for the pages ahead.)

Janice, through her work with the League of Women Voters, has earned the reputation of being a diligent, caring citizen, one who, when getting involved with an issue, studies it thoroughly and works tirelessly to get a program advanced or corrected, whichever effect is called for. A good many citizens have been looking at Janice as a possible village board candidate for a number of years now.

And now it's time for Janice to decide. Not just decide whether to run or not but, like Ike had to decide years ago, whether to run as a Democratic or a Republican candidate. You see, Janice has been regis-

tered as an independent and, in her town, even the most local of offices
are contested by candidates representing the two major national political parties.

Janice can't understand why a person can't run on her own merit.
She doesn't see how a party's national platform has anything to do with
an issue such as raising the parking fee at the train station. Yet the only
way Janice can run for the village board is under the aegis of either the
Republican or the Democratic party.

"Why," Janice asks Phil, "do people have to run *against* one another, rather than run *for* an office?"

And Phil answers, "Don't ask me."

Then, whom should Janice ask?

How about Him?

> God, sometimes I have the feeling
> That life is one big competition
> And You're the Supreme Spectator
> Watching us go at each other.
>
> But *must* we go at each other?
> Must this be a world of opposing forces
> At every level of life?
> I understand that
> Conflicts are bound to arise
> Between the forces of good and evil,
> But help me to understand, Dear God,
> Why there have to be conflicts
> Between good and good.

Janice's chances of winning the election, no matter which party en-
dorses her, are slimmer than they should be. Janice, as noted, is quite
able. She is also quite popular. But Janice doesn't have "the killer instinct." Whether it's politics or tennis, Janice doesn't "go for the jugu-
lar." She is primarily interested in communicating her point, not hum-
bling her opponent. She cares more about the fluidity of her ground
strokes, not in winning the match. It's not that Janice is not capable of
"putting her opponent away." She sees no point in it.

Ironic, isn't it, that Janice should be considered lacking something
because she is not all that competitive? The meek may inherit the earth,
but they won't win a village election.

Unlike Janice, the majority of us crave competition and actually thrive on it. Just look at what happens in our microcosmic suburban world around election time. Some of the humblest people ever to bring out the trash on Wednesday and whip up a bunch of brownies on Saturday morning begin thinking of themselves as political kingmakers. People whose only influence, only "pull" heretofore was getting extra cheese on their pizza without being charged for it, all of a sudden fancy themselves to be mighty power brokers.

Time was that in townships the string pullers were the hometown attorneys who had a vested interest in local government. (Invariably they *wore* vests too.) Now television has made Mark Hannas of us all. Now the druggist thinks he can be a whiz of a campaign manager. The high school English teacher believes she can plot out the political upset of the decade. The hairdresser fancies himself to be the most effective fund-raiser this side of Pennsylvania Avenue.

What gets into us?

Probably the system.

The political system is glorified for us in the media. The tube stokes our dreams, and, God knows, dreaming is one of the most joyous joys of the human condition. We dream new roles for ourselves. We assume, for whatever period, different personae.

Is it true in your town? The local political scene breeds local political specialists. Now not only can one be a campaign manager devising a strategy that can catapult a virtual unknown into the inexplicably coveted town clerk's seat, but one can also be adept at a single ploy, one particular specialty, that just might swing the entire election.

And just who are these specialists and what are their roles?

There is the Pamphleteer. This person may be a working ad man, the editor of the high school yearbook, or a homemaker with the ability to spell. The Pamphleteer will first come up with a pithy but strained rhyme, e.g., "Forge ahead . . . elect George instead." The Pamphleteer will then list the candidate's assets and affiliations, cataloging every civic group imaginable with whom George has had the slightest connection. The Pamphleteer will search for a novel typeface, something strikingly distinctive—and usually very difficult to read. The Pamphleteer will not settle for the expected head shot of George. No, he will paste together a montage of George at the sewerage treatment plant, at the train station, at a senior citizens potluck supper. Then the Pamphleteer, bursting with civic and creative pride, will present his layout to the local party overseers, only to have that group ask him to redo the piece using that hauntingly familiar line—"It's time for a change."

The Balloonist is the promotion biggie, the person with the knack of getting a political message across on a personal, hand-to-hand, face-to-face level. That, of course, requires balloons. Balloons are essential. Everyone perceives that. Ah, but the *color* of the balloon has to set the candidate apart from competition. Red and blue? They're the patriotic colors. But everyone uses red and blue. George's balloons must be magenta or puce, some distinctive, proprietary shade. The Balloonist also doubles as Bumper Chief, Poster Promoter and Bagman. No, not *that* kind of bagman. It appears that more and more local candidates are getting their promises out in front of the public via plastic shopping bags. The bags are reusable. They are strong and durable. They can hold the heft of three medium-sized cantaloupes. They are carried around by people, many of whom are senior citizens, who otherwise wouldn't be caught dead lugging around someone's advertising message. Ad bags are today's sandwich boards. And today the Balloonist et al. are so into their work, so energetic, that they have no concept at all of the postelection flotsam they have left around the community. Flotsam? Why flotsam? Couldn't it be treasure? Who knows? Someday a magenta George balloon may be worth as much to a collector as an Alf Landon button.

The Pourer is the hostess who fancies herself the Perle Mesta of her generation. Of course, if she didn't star in *Call Me Madam* in her high school musical, the hostess wouldn't have the foggiest idea who Perle Mesta was. Not only does the Pourer arrange a coffee whereat her neighbors can meet George, hear his views, and ask some questions, but the Pourer all too frequently tends to go overboard with her hostessing. Since there are any number of coffees by any number of different Pourers during the campaign, an especially motivated Pourer will spend an afternoon and then some baking plum tortes or crafting little watercress and muenster-cheese finger sandwiches or some such thing that will make her coffee for George stand out from other coffees for George. Unfortunately, candidate George will be the one to gobble up most of the plum torte, leaving little or nothing for his constituents to nibble on.

The Baiter is that indispensable campaign worker who flits from one candidate forum to another asking supposedly embarrassing questions of the opposition candidate. The opposition candidate is seldom embarrassed by the Baiter's questions, however, since they are more or less the same questions *his* Baiter intends to ask *his* opponent. To succeed as a Baiter, one must have a certain voice quality. It should be distinctive and penetrating. The best Baiters have a voice quality that is a laryngeal hybrid of Barbara Walters and Mick Jagger.

If truth be told, I have sat in meetings with all these specialists. If the *whole* truth be told, I have been the Pamphleteer. And if *nothing but* the truth be told, I have relished playing the role of a king- and queen-maker.

Is there anything wrong with that?

Well, not really.

But have I shown my gratitude?

Gratitude for what?

For the role.

The role?

The role.

> Thank you, Almighty God, for allowing me
> To achieve even more than the Army promises.
> The Army, as You know, tells people
> To "be all that you can be";
> You, however, allow us
> To be all that *they* can be,
> Giving us the chance,
> Even for a brief week or two,
> To assume roles and dreams and postures
> Of other creations of Yours.
> I thank You, God, for the roles
> You've allowed me to perform from time to time,
> But let me thank You most of all, Father,
> For my favorite role:
> Me.

*　*　*

The phrase is shouted almost in unison. It comes from B.J.'s room. It comes from Jennifer's room. It's darn near stereophonic. The phrase comes as a baleful blast, and it's repeated almost exponentially as children grow from toddlerhood to teens.

"I'M BORED!"

"I'm bored," whines Jennifer.

"I'm bored," screams B.J.

And from some distant parental hideaway in the house come a variety of responses.

"Read a book."

"Go watch TV."

"Have you finished your homework?"

It is a verifiable fact that nearly everyone in America under the age of eighteen nowadays (some put the age as high as *twenty*-eight) tends to have the temperament of a gerbil. Everyone in that age category craves constant activity, instant gratification, 'round-the-clock amusement. Whether that craving is normal to the maturation process or whether it's in any way beneficial to one's development is not the issue here. The issue is that an adult's answer to "I'm bored" is more often than not "Go do something—*by yourself.*" Those three suggestions offered to B.J. and Jennifer, for example—read a book, watch television and (ugh!) do homework—are exhortations for the youngsters to go off and do something—alone.

If we were able to translate "I'm bored" into what it actually means, into its implicit implication, our response to the plaint might be altogether different.

So what does "I'm bored" really mean?

It means, "Entertain me."

Boredom frequently stems from a form of undiagnosed loneliness. Those repetitive cries from the kids just may be thinly veiled—and not so thinly, actually—cries for togetherness.

When the children were smaller, Phil might have snapped at them, "Bored? How in the world can you be bored? You have so many things to play with!"

Things, yes. But how about *people?* Aren't people more entertaining than things?

The success of Trivial Pursuit was not just because we as a society became intensely interested in the esoterica of yesteryear, but that we could *share* that nostalgia in a communal memory-jogging competitive way. We were *together.* The pursuit may have been trivial, but the opportunity to be with somebody was significant indeed. The game wasn't really entertaining us. The game was a device by which we were entertaining each other.

The longtime success of Monopoly can't possibly be attributed to our rapturous pleasure in building hotels on Baltic and Mediterranean. Monopoly, homophonically speaking, could have been the ultimate bored game. Yet generations of people have loved playing Monopoly, because, although a thin and now outdated concept, it offers us a chance to be together, to entertain one another, to combat loneliness.

With all the appositives given to God throughout recorded, and no doubt *pre*-recorded, time, has anyone either petitioned Him or praised Him as The Great Entertainer?

Has any "bored" child had the wonderfully naïve intuition to say, "Wanna play with me, God?"

Has an incipient adult ever had the audacious humility to say, "Listen, God, I've got nothing planned for tonight. How about You? Want to get together and do something tonight?"

A thought. Just a thought.

TUESDAY MORNING

Loving Lists and Noodging Notes

Family members sharing a suburban roof can go for days without seeing one another for more than an hour or two. Here's a scenario that's all too familiar: Phil takes the 6:33 into the city, showering, shaving, dressing and leaving for the station before anyone else in the house has left pillow and percale.

Jennifer gets picked up for school at 7:30 by her hunk-of-the-month, Tony, whose glowing reputation among Jennifer's girlfriends is not in the least tainted by the fact that Tony has a car! Tony picks up Jennifer a minute or two before B.J. gets out of bed to get ready for his 8:15 school bus.

Janice, no longer plagued by the guilt that for generations had mothers force-feeding piping hot breakfasts into their children, wakes around eight. She checks on B.J. to make sure he's taken his vitamins and packed *all* of his schoolbooks. Reassured, she sends him off to his screechy school bus.

(Do school buses come factory-equipped with brakes that screech? Are the brakes made that way intentionally so the kids will hear the bus coming and they'll come running? Or maybe they are made with the built-in screech so that other drivers will hear the bus and stop their vehicles in accordance with the law. Whatever the case, it's strange that when you hear a school bus that *doesn't* screech, you think there's something wrong with it.)

The family whose members have scattered at different times and to different places does not, as a rule, gather as a unit at dinnertime, either. Jennifer, for example, may have a field-hockey game (away, not home— why is it more games are scheduled away, rather than home?) so she won't be back until seven-thirty at the very earliest.

Janice has a hospice meeting at Ames Memorial at seven, and she probably won't be back home until sometime after nine. B.J. has a scout meeting after school and then a pizza party, and he'll be dropped off at home by the scoutmaster sometime after eight.

Phil? Oh, he's off on an overnight business trip to Cincinnati. He won't be back until tomorrow night.

This family chronology is not uncommon. And it's made even more complicated should the mother have a job as well as the father.

Some sociologists believe that all this scurrying about has seriously frayed the very fiber of family life. Some claim that our lack of sufficient face-to-face communication has weakened relationships among family members. To these people I say, "But don't forget: God created magnetism."

To which people respond, "You must be off your non-sequitur rocker!"

I defend myself this way: One of the by-products of the creation of the universe, no matter to what scientific theory you happen to subscribe, is magnetism, specifically the tremendous influence of the earth's magnetic poles. Without listing all the remarkable inventions based on magnetism, let me mention what may be mankind's—and especially suburban mankind's—most important invention: *the kitchen magnet.*

Thanks to the kitchen magnet, and its divinely decreed power to hold notes to metallic cabinets and doorjambs, and most especially to the refrigerator, our family relationships can be full, rich and loving although we have been temporarily removed from one another's physical presence.

In fact, baring our feelings is frequently much easier with a note attached to the refrigerator than it is in a face-to-egg-all-over-one's-face situation. The language and tone we use in those notes says more than any factual information we're trying to impart. A dimension of our humanity—its frailty, its wonder—is exposed up there on the old canary yellow Frigidaire. Consider the refrigerator as sort of a scoreboard of the soul. We can use that scoreboard compassionately and creatively to communicate our love and respect for one another.

Jennifer, for example, will use notes to apologize for things she otherwise has difficulty apologizing for. Janice uses notes to give orders with an unbossy lovingness, something the natural inflection of her voice is not always able to convey. B.J. uses notes for inventive deviltry. Phil uses them, in his uniquely cornball way, to show affection.

There is something about the formation of the sounds "sor" and "ree" and the expulsion of those sounds from her mouth that Jennifer finds particularly painful. So the teenager puts her regrets to paper and then attaches that paper, with a magnetized animal or magnetized representation of a fried egg, onto the fridge. One time it may be a note that reads:

> To Mom and Dad,
> From Jen.
> Unscramble the following letters
> to discover an important message.
> R   O   R   Y   S

Another time, Jennifer may express her feelings over the same sort of adolescent intemperateness with a multiple-choice question that reads:

> Jennifer is:
> a. a dope;
> b. inconsiderate;
> c. sorry;
> d. all of the above.

It's not that this family is any more verbal than the average family. Perhaps it's *less* verbal. Janice has trouble spelling; B.J. was diagnosed as being dyslexic and has been having remedial help since he was in the second grade, and Phil, Jr. (away at college), speaks primarily in grunts. No, this is not an especially gifted verbal family. It's just one that has discovered that taking a minute or two to jot down one's thoughts—and sometimes, emotions—can mean a great deal to the people on the reading end of those considerately and/or passionately conceived messages.

Janice, for example, not only dispenses instructions on her notes to the family, but she has a habit of codiciling rewards at the ends of her messages. B.J. might find a note from his mother that says: "Please clean your room. It's a pigpenn. There's rassberry sherbert in the freezer." And Jennifer has been known to find notes from Mom like

"Put your towle back in the bathroom after shower. I bought you gel. In linen closet."

B.J., whose communication skills have not been academically buffed yet, has nonetheless sharpened his sense of humor to a fiendishly whetted edge. Members of the family may traipse into the kitchen on some morning and find a note from B.J. stuck to the refrigerator that reads, "Has anyone seen the frog I brought home from school yesterday?"

Of all the family members, Phil fancies himself as both the creative and the romantic creature of the five. Some years ago, he had read that Red Skelton wrote a new song for his wife every single day. Knowing he didn't quite have that kind of talent, Phil decided to knock out a few lines of doggerel to his wife, if not daily, then whenever the muse moved him. Janice has stashed away packets of Phil's verse, since the Ogden Nash who shares her life and home has been doing this for years now. Phil rather hoped Janice would save his pieces. After all, they are, if not literary standouts, thoughtful and timely.

> February 15.
> In 1812 on this day Charles Tiffany was born,
> A man with considerable marketing tools,
> Who never understood that his lot in life
> Would be to keep you, my dear, in jewels.

And then Phil wrote:

> March 14.
> Though the creator of Dennis the Menace was born
>   on this day
> He deserves no laudatory rhymes . . .
> No, I'd rather sing the praises of a woman
> Who created menaces three different times!

Phil's verses give him a chance to wax somewhat amorous. The poetry is not Byronic, to be sure. Nor even Judith Viorst. But no one can argue that, in its fashion, the poetry isn't very very loving.

> July 6.
> Today I just may give you bites on the neck . . .
> Now, what does this unbridled passion mean?
> That in 1885 on this very day
> Pasteur discovered rabies vaccine.

Strained? Who's to say what's strained when a person tries to communicate something from the heart? Being affectionate may at times call for something nonsensical.

> December 29.
> To compare your sexiness with Madame Pompadour's
> I surely wouldn't dare;
> Although it's that lady's birthday. Janice,
> I prefer the way you do *your* hair.

It is a little-discussed and not well-documented fact that muses are rare nowadays. Writers are much more willing to give inspirational credit to a particular brand of vodka or a trendy drug than they are to a person, be that person mythical or even human. God as muse, an idea that may have had support and cachet in certain mountainside caves centuries ago, certainly hasn't received much attention in literary circles in recent years. (Eros as muse is probably the only mythic creature having any success in literary circles.) Literati would hardly consider the Janices and Phils and Jennifers who dash off bits of loving doggerel, or lines of familial caring, to be worthy of reflection and review. Yet the efforts of those family members, whether you consider a note on the refrigerator to have literary import or not, have a poignant effect on the reader of that message 100 percent of the time. Now, where is there a writer who wouldn't give his very automatic correction capability to have that sort of response to *his* work?

Those refrigerator notes are mini-manifestations of our humanity, love and guilt, hope and fear, sharing and joy, and there's only one conceivable muse who can evoke that wide and wonderful an array of literary emotions.

TUESDAY AFTERNOON

What's Your Handicap? God.

It is considerably easier to have a thought about—and perhaps a word with—God in the city than it is in the suburbs. Yes, the suburbs are generally quieter and that should facilitate Godthoughts. But there are more hints of God, more opportunities to bring him to mind in the city, than there are in the burbs.

You may pass a bag lady on a city street corner and mutter to yourself, "God bless her, what a pitiful creature!" Why, God might think you are actually talking to Him and not to yourself, and He might choose to answer you.

In the city you may also stroll past any number of places of worship, one or more of which may jolt your consciousness a bit to remind you of the deity honored therein. Then there are the sidewalk evangelists all too eager to remind you of an eternity either with or without God, those options pointed out to you in loud and colorful polarizations. If you're walking with a friend or business associate at the time and you are struck by one of those examples just mentioned, you might even elaborate on some aspect of God and your relationship with Him to your strollmate.

But if you are waiting for the foursome just ahead of you to putt out and move off the green, and you happen to say to your playing partner while biding time, "It must be tough for those people in the slums of

Calcutta to believe in God," your partner will give you a look of quizzical anguish and that unequivocally unrewarding expression "Huh?"

"Well," you'll be all too willing to explain, "I just finished reading Lapierre's *City of Joy,* and it's all about the squalor of Calcutta, and I was thinking . . ."

And you stand in glaring danger of being labeled a religious nut. Your golf buddy will be thinking he's playing a round with some sort of Godfreak, someone who must be out of his cerebral gourd to bring up God right here smack dab in the middle of the fairway. Both Malcolm Muggeridge and William Buckley have written about social situations in which they mentioned God and were greeted with silence . . . cringing silence.

There is a very logical explanation for this disquieting quietude. Most people think there is a place for God. Those same people believe there are places where God is *in*appropriate. That means it is gauche to speak of Him in certain places and situations.

Emily Dickinson wrote, "They say God is everywhere and yet we always think of him as somewhat of a recluse."

Coming from the hardly outgoing Emily, the statement is a wee bit ironic, but nevertheless true. And that's too bad. Amherst is a lovely town. Some might even consider it a suburb of sorts. And yet Emily's fellow townsfolk, to the poet's way of thinking, didn't consider God there neighbor. Some communities actually find that recluses within their town limits are quaint conversation pieces. In the burbs, however, there's such pressure to socialize (weekends are booked solid with social events) that it's impossible for the most determined of recluses to establish his lonely digs there.

So, to the majority of suburbanites, God isn't really a recluse. Neither is He as frequently perceived to be as ubiquitous as He is. Is God in the sand trap? Is He at the bridge table, or playing the net? As sure as you're there, He's there.

Consider the sand trap, for example. While you're there waggling your wedge waiting for the remainder of the foursome (all with much better, no-problem lies) to hit up, God, part of your fivesome says to you, "What are you doing?"

"You know what I'm doing here. I'm here because I thought I could reach the green with a seven iron, rather than a six iron, that's what I'm doing here."

"I know that. I mean, how are you going to make the most of this situation?"

"Oh, I don't know . . . wrong . . . I *do* know . . . I'm going to take my sand wedge, open up the face a bit and blast the living . . ."

And then it dawns on you that that's not quite what God had in mind. So now, somewhat enlightened, you respond:

> Father, thank You for giving Your creations
> The gift of *re*-creation, too.
> I appreciate Your reminder
> That I have an obligation to make
> The day enjoyable for those around me.
> So that, rather than grousing
> About being in the trap,
> Rather than ranting and raving
> About *my* game and *my* predicament,
> I'll turn my attention
> To my playing partners
> And talk about *their* game,
> Accepting my impending double bogey
> With a grin of good will.
> (But tell me, God,
> Can a grin of good will
> Be grinned through
> Clenched teeth?)

I had long thought that the most difficult chore that God could possibly be faced with in His abundantly graced suburbs was to sit in on a weekly bridge game. Not because of the conversation around the bridge table, which generally doesn't have much to do with the game itself, rather with certain of God's creatures, e.g., Helen, who's going to Weight Watchers; Al and Annette, who are splitting up; Betty Randall, who may or may not be pregnant and may or may not be happy about it.

No, there's plenty of interest in humanity at the bridge table to keep God occupied. It's the game itself. I thought God would be monumentally bored with bridge. Why? It's the sameness of the game. Bridge is monotonous: the conventions, the prescribed plays, the pro forma bids, the running of trumps, the declaration of honors, the rote that passes for fun.

But should God, He of all, be bored by sameness? God, who has watched millennia tick by, centuries upon centuries of sameness? Of course not.

Sameness needn't automatically be considered boring; sameness can quite often provide a welcome sense of security. But to break up the confounded sameness of bridge, wouldn't it be nice if one day a player looked at her cards, sighed despondently, "God, what a hand!" and was answered by a celestial whisper, "Lead with a diamond."

Of all the fun-and-alleged-games at which God's presence is required, tennis is quite probably the most critical. And one form of tennis above all: mixed doubles. No other single sport that's regularly played in suburbia roils up ill feelings, gives rise to such horrific pomposity and threatens relationships the way mixed doubles does.

Consider the conversations that spring from those combinations.

Husband playing with Wife will tend to instruct ("Toss the ball higher"), direct ("Watch the alley") and chastize ("What a dumb time to lob!").

Husband playing with Non-Wife will tend to applaud ("Lovely backhand"), exhort ("We'll break 'em right back") and forgive ("Lotta topspin on that ball; *I* woulda had trouble with *that* one").

Wife playing with Husband will tend to reprimand ("Don't tell me what to do"), demand ("Stay on your side") and dismiss ("But it's only a game, Phil").

Wife playing with Non-Husband will tend to be coy ("I've only been playing for three years"), supportive ("Great overhead, Harry!") and will relish victory ("Did we ever sock it to them!") the way she never did with her husband. And she's not even a very competitive person!

But the structure of the game is such that God just can't stroll onto the court and ask, "Mind if I hit with you?" The hour and a half of mixed doubles will just have to run its caustic course without the intervention of the premier peacemaker. And, depending on the severity of the spleen being vented, that can prove to be catastrophic.

But a thought. Just a thought. Everybody is familiar with the now-cliché TV shot before a college football game. No, you cynics, not the one of the alums handing over the monthly allotment checks to the players—the one with the entire team gathered along the sideline, huddled around the coach, beefy arms around beefy bodies, heads bent, all praying together for victory, no crippling knee injuries, and whatever else may seem appropriate.

Well, imagine if, just before a mixed-doubles tennis match, the four people involved, as they unzipped their racket covers, popped open a can of balls and slipped on their designer headbands, clustered together at the net and said:

> Before we start serving and smashing and lobbing,
> We ask You to help us, O Father above,
> To play at our best, but never forgetting
> Friendship means more than six-love.

I can't get this vision out of my head. Would that *Sports Illustrated* would photograph it (if it ever happened) and run it as a four-color spread. It's an aerial view looking down on eight tennis courts of a posh suburban country club. At the net on each court, huddled closely together, are four players reciting the Mixed Doubles Pre-Match Prayer.

TUESDAY NIGHT

Here's Grandma, There's Alex, Where's Inky?

Census-taking has to be one of the most imprecise, if not totally futile, of government activities. Not a science, mind you, an activity. Just an activity. The doorbell ringer or questionnaire analyzer may think he knows how many people live at 31 Earle Street, but he hasn't any idea of the human traffic that stops there for a day, a week, or even some lengthier, indeterminate period of time.

The suburban home, because of its comfort or convenience (also known as a spare bedroom) is a way station of sorts. The owners of the house, figuratively and in many cases literally, stand at the front door in various postures of welcome. Do you read body language? Notice how few welcomers open their arms expansively in a wide and genuine sign of "Come in, come in, we're so happy to have you." More often, the arms are loosely or tightly folded, a symbolic if not actual "bar-the-door" gesture. Seeing that the sleep-over guests are body-language illiterate and keep trooping in, the host and hostess then slowly unfold their arms and extend at least one in a wave of "This way, come right in this way."

Some of those guests come invited, others unexpectedly. Some spread joy; others spread out on the sofa.

Our acceptance of these people (and animals, too) and our willingness to share our home with them is one of the great

    a. benefits;

b. obligations;

c. challenges of our suburban life.

Consider for a moment the benefits, obligations and challenges of a visit by Grandma.

"I hope I'm not putting you out. It's been a while since I saw the children and I thought . . ."

"Well, Mother, I don't know how much of the children you're going to see. B.J. is off on a trip with the chorus. Jennifer has been doing volunteer work at the hospital after school and, you know, Phil Junior won't be home from college for a few weeks yet.

"Yes," says Grandma with a wise, septuageneric smile, "but I consider *you* my children too."

Now Janice and Phil feel awful. Their initial reaction upon Grandma's appearance (graciously unstated) was that her visit would put a serious crimp in their own long-planned social schedule. ("Do we bring Mother to the Bentleys', the concert, the clambake?") But when the lady allows (alludes, really) that she's come to visit out of a combination of love and loneliness (the *combination* that actually makes the world go 'round) Phil and Janice feel guilty. As they should.

Can Grandma assimilate into suburban life for the length of her stay? In truth, the length of her stay will hinge on her ability to assimilate into suburban life. As for joining her *adult* children at their social engagements, Grandma has no problem with that at all. She finds the Bentleys delightful, the concert pleasant (at least the part she's awake for). And the clambake? "Jingles, that was fun," is her review of it.

No, it's not the social life her family leads that Grandma finds difficult to take, it's the home life. Grandma finds their home life so frenzied. Everybody coming and going. Nobody sitting down for a few minutes to relax. All the hustle. All the scurry. No one eating breakfast. Can they really be happy running around as they do? wonders Grandma from her vantage point, her constant and only vantage point: a chair in the kitchen. Throughout her stay at her children's home, Grandma rarely leaves her kitchen chair.

Now, Grandma's perspective, if not her location, can't be dismissed. Nor should it be dismissed. It just may be that this lady and thousands of other women and men in her chronological stage of life are periodically sent into the suburbs by God on a mission. That mission: slow up life.

No matter how full a schedule, how hectic a week, Janice and Phil may have planned, they are not so insensitive that they won't find time to sit and chat and eat and reminisce with Grandma. With some effort, heroic to be sure, they may even get Grandma to move from her kitchen chair into the living room. And whether she realizes it or not, Grandma will have succeeded, at least for the time being, in decelerating her children's high-speed lifestyle.

There's another wonderful service Grandma's periodic visits provide. Besides slowing up her suburban beloveds, Grandma *humbles.* This woman, who years ago blew up little Phil's balloons, now does a masterful job of bursting them.

Consider the fact that a good many of today's suburbanites, probably an overwhelming majority of them, didn't come from the suburbs. They worked their way up to the suburbs and the real estate bragging rights that go along with that move. So when, one night at dinner, Phil says, "Mother, would you like a little Beaujolais, the new Beaujolais is just in," it's understandable that Grandma responds, "Beaujowhat? Wine? Wine with meatloaf?"

"It's not *meatloaf.* It's a *veal* and *pork* loaf straight out of last Thursday's *Times,* and a nice new Beaujolais is perfectly appropriate with . . ."

"Your father used to have a Schlitz with *his* meatloaf."

POP! There goes another balloon.

In suburbia, humility just doesn't go with the territory. After all, suburbia is synonymous with achievement, and achievement, no matter how hard we may fight it, has its affectations. That's why a Grandma, a vocal and candid and refreshingly honest reminder of our roots, is so important. Her ilk simply can't be bilked. Her eyes may be failing somewhat, but she can sure see through a bottle of Beaujolais. Especially Beaujolais with meatloaf!

Grandma's mission has worked, more or less. At least part of it has. Now when the shout from one of the kids announces, "Here's Grandma," Phil shelves his suburban pretensions for the duration of her stay. He is working on shelving them for even longer, but that's difficult. Difficult for him. Difficult for all of us.

*   *   *

"There's Alex!" shrieks Jennifer as her friend varooms into the driveway. Varooming is just one of the reasons Janice and Phil feel queasy about Alex spending the week with them. Alex and Alex's parents have

different values from Janice and Phil. Alex is just about the same age as
Jennifer. Alex is allowed to drive a moped. That's the varoom.

Alex is also permitted to smoke and address adults by their first
names. She also received notoriety in her high school and her local
newspaper last year when her essay *Bisexuality: An Idea Whose Time
Has Come"* won third prize in some sort of national magazine competition.

But how do you say no when people (specifically your own daughter
and the neighbors down the street) ask if a child can spend the week at
your house as those neighbors go off to a business convention? Certainly
Janice and Phil don't know how to say no to that.

"Yes, Alex can stay with us, Jennifer, but she has to understand the
house rules."

And when little Alex, just two weeks older than her own Jennifer,
says to Janice, "Oh yeah, Janice, I catch your drift. No screwin' around.
Sure. Okay. I can live by your law for the doo-ration," Janice's only
recourse is not to Phil, who has already stomped off to the bedroom
asking himself why they had agreed to Alex's stay in the first place, but
to God:

> Isn't it strange how I tolerate
> The wildest habits and beliefs and values,
> Just so long as none of them are fostered under my roof?
> No, *You* probably don't think it strange, God,
> Since You know so well the limitations of Your creatures.
> Well, it's time for me to ask for a higher form
>   of forbearance, Father,
> One that permits me to abide those values I find
>   unacceptable
> For my own life and those lives most important to me.
> Help keep me and my house open enough
> That I may better understand
> The lifestyles of others,
> And they may appreciate
> The value of mine.
> Amen.

* * *

A survey done by one Victoria Lea Voith and presented to the American Veterinarian Medical Association found that 89 percent of cats

sometimes sleep with their owners and that 97 percent of cats greet their owners at the door. Had Ms. Voith interviewed B.J. for her survey, those percentages might have been even a tad higher. B.J. and Inky slept together more often than not. Inky greeted B.J. at the door almost every night, even with B.J.'s strange homecoming hours. That door was important to Inky. It was the door outside of which, many months before, Inky was found meowing. Inky wasn't Inky then. He was a scrawny stray all-black, very-male cat. Shortly thereafter he became less scrawny, less-male and Inky. Inky's attachment to B.J. and B.J.'s reciprocity made the loss of Inky all that much more difficult to handle.

How *did* the loss happen?

A little background.

Their nighttime routine was always the same. Just before bedtime, B.J. would let Inky out the back door for his evening toilette. B.J. would then go off to bed, his parents letting in the cat in about a half hour. Inky would then skedaddle up the stairs, into B.J.'s bedroom and up on his bed, nestling himself alongside the by-now fast asleep child. That was the drill every single night . . . until the night Inky didn't return.

The reaction was as quick, as caring, as it would be to a calamity involving hundreds and hundreds of people. Phil took to the flashlight. He searched, at first systematically, and then frantically, for the cat. Then he drove around the neighborhood, waving the flashlight out the window. Twice he drove, inadvertently, up on neighbors' lawns, because his eyes and flashlight were riveted on where Inky might have, just might have, been. No sign. No trace.

And then B.J., waking up in the middle of the night, groped for his pet, and not finding him, called out to his parents, "Where's Inky? Where's Inky?"

The sorrow and the grieving that followed are painfully familiar to hundreds of pet owners. For weeks thereafter, B.J., Phil, too, for that matter, wandered through the neighborhood and beyond, far beyond, oh so plaintively calling, "Iiiiiinnnnky . . . Iiiinnnnky . . . here Innnnky."

The cat never returned.

That may, in fact, be one of the saddest four-word sentences in our language: the cat never returned.

What is this attachment we have for all those four-legged creatures we feed, walk, and brush? Why and how do we reach such levels of passion for our pets that we cannot seem to reach with so many human beings?

Why?

Because pets *respond to us*. They greet us at the door; they snuggle up to us. They even listen quietly and attentively to our troubles. (That survey also found that 57 percent of owners talked to their cats about important matters.) With the warmth and effusiveness of response we get from cats and dogs and an occasional bird, it's little wonder we cherish their friendship so much and mourn their loss so grievously.

Do you suppose if we received a similar response from more human beings we could be as fervent in our attachment to them as we are to the Inkys and Dukes and Tweeties of our lives?

And what if we reacted to people in the same warm, trusting and naïve way that pets do? Would we earn the same measure of devotion from these people that their pets have? And one final question: isn't it worth a try?

WEDNESDAY MORNING

Carless in Camelot

Gallant steeds met the transportation needs of people living in idyllic kingdoms of yore. Rarely, if ever, was any household a one-steed family. Transportation—in this case, hoofs—had to be in abundant supply and readily accessible.

The same holds true for our latter-day idyllic kingdom. Transportation—in our case, wheels—has to be available for every adult and a good percentage of not-quite-adults. A one-car family in suburbia is the exception, not the rule.

Our dependence on today's sheet-metal steeds (has any automaker ever considered the name "Gallant" for one of his models?) is probably a matter of status and time, rather than of pure necessity. Save for the suburbs of a couple of metropoloi such as Los Angeles and Detroit, most American suburbs are walkable. Yet a resident of Scarsdale, Smoke Rise or Shaker Heights seen *walking* to pick up a sweater at the dry cleaner's would be as startling as seeing a knight *walking* in search of the Holy Grail.

In this twentieth-century Camelot, cars are required to whisk us off to our appointed rounds. We say, we claim, we rationalize that we cannot afford the luxury of a fifteen-minute stroll to the Spiffy Jiffy Cleaners. We don't say, we don't claim, but deep-down we know that we must also be seen and cataloged and cherished in the makes and models of cars we drive. (Remember Janice's Jaguar aspirations.) So we rely on our pair (or more) of cars. In fact, we rely so much on them that when those cars become unavailable we find it difficult to cope.

Tuesday night, for instance, Janice said to Phil, "I'm taking the Honda in for its inspection tomorrow."

Phil said to Janice, "Want me to follow you down? You can leave the Honda, drive me to the station, and take my Buick."

"No," said Janice, "that'll be too early for me. I'll just wait for the car. Inspections don't take long."

And so it happened that Janice did take the Honda to the dealer about 9 A.M. Wednesday for its annual inspection, expecting it to be a pro forma affair. But the inspection didn't run according to forma. The service manager said to Janice, "Gee, lady, you're goin' to have to leave the car here for a while. The wheels are way outa line and your muffler's shot, to boot. There's some work to do."

"But *I've* got work to do too. I've got a very busy schedule today. How long is it going to take?"

"Oh, 'bout two, three hours. You're fifth in line."

"Fifth in line?" Janice squeals in that acerbic squeal of hers as she rushes off to phone Phil. She intends to tell her husband that she'll take a cab to the train station, where Phil has left the Buick, pick up the Buick for the day, and Phil can call her when he's coming home from the city and she'll come to the station to pick him up.

Good plan. But, good grief! Phil, at nine-fifteen, isn't at the office yet. Phil, who is always in the office by seven-thirty every workday morning, still isn't there this morning and it's well after nine. Devoted secretary, Mary Jane, tells frantic wife, Janice, "He isn't in yet."

"Isn't in yet?" that same rhetorically interrogative squeal of Janice's now has a bit of a panic pitch to it. "But I didn't hear of any train delays on the morning news. What could be . . . well . . . well . . . when he comes in have him . . . eh . . . call me at the . . . at the Honda dealer."

And just where *is* Phil? Symbiotically, at Joe's Car Repair. It seems that, halfway to the train station, Phil felt his Buick losing speed going up the hill. Fortunately, he had to pass his repairman of long standing, the ever reliable Joe, who, unfortunately and unreliably, wasn't in yet. So Phil, naturally concerned about his car, waited for Joe and missed his train and the four trains that followed.

Joe's initial diagnosis, once he *did* arrive, was "Looks like dirty plugs. I'll blow 'em out and have you out of here in no time flat." No time flat turned about to be about nine-twenty. And Phil and Buick were not on their way. Joe announced the chilling news "Nope . . . it ain't the plugs, it's the clutch."

"It's the clutch?" Phil, who had grown to share so much with his wife, now even shared her interrogative squeal. The squeal sounded silly coming out of Phil's mouth, however.

And so Janice and Phil sat (or, more accurately, paced) in separate automotive service establishments, ten miles apart. Their cars had come to standstills; so had their worlds.

Rather than reflect on the emotions of Janice and Phil as they fume, whine, shout, pout, remonstrate, ululate, and lament their plights, let's consider the opportunity that *Godglitches* give us. Oh, sure, Phil might be wont to blame somebody on a General Motors assembly line for installing a faulty clutch, and Janice may find it hard to believe that the muffler on her car could go so soon, and maybe the dealer is trying to make a few extra bucks claiming she needs a new muffler when she really doesn't. These are logical thoughts. It's natural that we, who have been blamed for things since birth, like to go through life blaming right back. But what if we could suspend this natural inclination every so often and, rather than instantly instinctively blaming someone or something, chalk up our unhappy situation to a Godglitch, a downtime of modest discomfort and inconvenience that allows us to perfect our humanity a bit.

How?

For example, once Phil's heartbeat and blood pressure subside to a more normal level, he might say to Joe as the repairman works on the car, "How's your son, Joe? The one I used to see helping you out here on Saturdays?"

"Oh, that's Pete, my oldest. He's studying for the cops, you know. Wants to be a trooper."

"That's great, just great, Joe."

"Yeah, but between you and me, I'm worried about the kid."

"Worried about what?"

"Well, me and the Mrs. have noticed Pete polishes off a six-pack just about every night. And that's at home. Who knows how much beer he's putting away outside the house? I mean, there's nothing wrong about a beer or two—but a six-pack every night?"

And although Phil is far from a counselor, he can show compassion and understanding, talking about his own Phil Jr., away at college, an

environment which, as both legend and reality have it, is highly condu-
cive to considerable beer drinking.

"Tell me, Joe . . . does your boy have any interests . . . I mean
other than the cops? Does he play ball, bowl, fish? Maybe he drinks all
that beer because he doesn't have much else to do?"

And they talk, the business executive and the car repairman, about
sons and fears and ambitions and alcoholism. Phil has managed to
forget about time and the clutch and the office. Joe is thrilled, relieved,
too, to be able to talk to somebody about his fears, especially here in the
shop, where he has been brooding about his son all alone for weeks
now.

Later Joe asks Phil, "Tell me, you work with any black people?"

"Oh, yes. We have quite a few. In fact I work very closely with a
black man in the research department. He heads up the division that
works directly with my division. What makes you ask?"

"Well, I've been so busy lately . . ."

"Don't knock it."

"I'm not, but it's been so busy I'm goin' to have to take on a mechanic to help me out three or four days a week. This black guy who
works down at the Shell station said he'd like to come work for me, but
I don't know. I'm not prejudice or nothing, but you hear so much about
work habits of blacks and how they just sometimes don't show up some
days without callin' . . ."

And Phil proceeds to give testimony, laced with facts, of the fine
performances of blacks with whom he's worked, convincing Joe, or so it
seems, that color and colored opinions shouldn't stand in the way of
hiring the man from the Shell station.

Phil's particular Godglitch—a clutch on the fritz—has given him the
time and the chance to polish up his humanness. He certainly didn't
intend to spend all that time chatting with Joe. Their conversation
slowed up the repairman. Yet Phil, as the time and the talk went on, no
longer seemed to care. He had even decided, somewhere in Hour Two,
to call it a day, and called his secretary to tell her so. "The day's half
over, Mary Jane. I don't think I'll bother coming in."

Meanwhile, in her suburban limbo, in the auto-service department of
her Honda dealer's, Janice paced, eyes darting from the watch on her
wrist to the clock on the wall, back to the watch on her wrist. The times
on both timepieces jibed—and ticked away at the same, and from
Janice's point of view, incredibly fast, rate of speed. She had already

missed her nail appointment. Now the lunch with Kathleen was in serious jeopardy. As Janice fished through her purse to find Kathleen's phone number to cancel lunch, she happened on a pack of notepaper she had bought at some organization benefit or other.

Janice's thought wasn't inspired—or was it? "Hmmm? I've got nothing better to do. Why not catch up on some correspondence?" She said this to herself more in resignation than in any burning desire to communicate with distant friends and relatives.

So she canceled lunch, took a rickety chair in the corner of the waiting room and proceeded to write letters to her college roommate, Sarah, who, now divorced, had after all these years decided to go back to school for her master's; her son Phil, Jr; her niece, also at college, but not very happy about it; Jane and Joe, who had been transferred to Japan; and her congresswoman, who had recently voted *for* aid to the Nicaraguan rebels.

Godglitched Janice was in the middle of a letter to Uncle Harold, in Boca Raton, recuperating from a hernia operation, when the service manager interrupted her note writing with, "Lady, your car is ready."

These moments of humanity-honing (in these cases, hours not moments) can't be programmed. They are spontaneous, because the actions that preceded them, the Godglitches, seem to be spontaneous. As spontaneous, say, as grace. Yet, being open to the possibility, being aware that you're experiencing not a minor catastrophe but an opportunistic Godglitch, just might prove wonderfully beneficial to you and a host of people in your sight—and in your memory.

WEDNESDAY AFTERNOON

Meditating Among the Marigolds,
Reflecting on the Roof

In the past couple of years, just about everything—and just about enough—has been written about the work ethic and the workaholic. *Just* about enough, but not *quite* enough. Has this ever been written? *The work ethic is a generally unassailable excuse that alleged workaholics use to stay away from home.*

"Generally unassailable?" Absolutely. The work ethic belongs in the apple-pie and motherhood impedestaled category. Who would ever knock it? Dedication to one's job, the determination to see an assignment through no matter what, is an idea that's unravelably woven into the fabric of our nation.

"Excuse," then? Again—absolutely. Would anyone argue that, given the same income for *not* working, most people would opt *not* to work, whether the work ethic is recognized as a basic good or not? Of course they would. The *pay* ethic prevails, not the *work* ethic. Yet the "alleged" workaholic ("alleged" because workaholism has been romanticized into a disease) claims that his (workaholism is also primarily attributed to men) drive is fueled by a zeal to do a job completely and well.

Is that why a brand manager must stay at his desk, checking on shampoo out-of-stocks in the Mid-Atlantic District until 11 o'clock night after night?

Is that why an attorney pores through his law-office library long after the "David Letterman Show" is over, not because the attorney has a particular case crunch, but for the "alleged" reason that he wants to familiarize himself on some particular marine-law issue? And he does this on a regular basis?

These very intelligent individuals, their reputations swathed in graduate sheepskins from the very best schools, can't possibly believe that they will be extolled and rewarded merely because they put in fourteen to sixteen hours a day. No. They are exploiting the interest in, and admiration of, workaholics, to hide, consciously or not, their disaffection or discomfort with home life.

This self-delusion is especially absurd when it comes to "alleged" workaholics at a high corporate level. These individuals believe their involvement must be virtually 'round-the-clock. The clock they assiduously avoid seeing is the one on their bedside night table.

Once, Phil, whose business career has progressed quite nicely, had to battle his desire to be labeled a workaholic and what he perceived as the adulation that went with the reputation. He saw some of his colleagues coming to work very early and staying very late. Metabolically a morning person, Phil himself has, for years, arrived at the office two hours prior to its official opening time. But somewhere along his career path Phil made the observation that his work (marketing) and most people's work, for that matter, didn't warrant the time, energy, and, more recently, the media attention they were being given.

This didn't mean Phil became a malingerer or a weekday afternoon golfer. It was just that Phil realized that work is a means to an end and not an end in itself. Is that conclusion nonoriental? A Westerner's conclusion? Or is the thought more spiritual than geographic?

At any rate, Phil felt not the least shiver of guilt as he drove his newly repaired Buick into his driveway on a Wednesday afternoon. He would spend the rest of his business day in a domestic way, taking care of the things that had to be done around the house. Around the outside of the house.

Have you noticed? Neighbors have this habit when they see you working outside: they feel obliged to come over and chat. As it happened, Phil's neighbor saw him at home and came over and spent most of the afternoon with him. And just what did Phil and God talk about?

Well, the garden, with all the recent rain, had grown aggravatingly beweeded. Phil, on all fours, groped his way around the pepper and cucumber plants, yanking at any and all vegetation that looked as though it could not bear zucchini. If it weren't for Janice's fondness for that vegetable, he would have yanked at the zucchini plants as well as the weeds. As it was, in his uprooting fervor Phil did occasionally pull up a marigold, a border of which had been planted around the vegetable garden because of that flower's purported ability to keep animals away. Something to do with the powerful and distinctive smell of the marigold.

Which prompted Phil to comment, "You know, God, You've created some pretty intriguing defense mechanisms. I mean, porcupine quills and turtle shells and this marigold smell . . ."

"And sleep."

"Sleep?"

"Yes," said God. "Have you noticed, Phil, how whenever there's a problem with one of the children, or some other family dilemma, financial or social, what do you do but . . . go to sleep?"

"I do?"

"You do. Sleep is *your* defense mechanism."

"Not a very realistic one, is it?"

"I didn't say that; you did."

Later Phil had to climb up on the roof. The maple tree and the pin oak had sent down seedlings and twigs that had then gathered in the gutters and around the drain spouts. Eavesdrippings. Phil is not wild about heights. He had trouble, as always, maintaining his balance as he scooped the arboreal detritus out of the gutters. The roof of his house isn't all that high or pitched all that steeply that Phil's acrophobia should reach high anxiety level. Phil's height terror is particularly agonizing when he's on a twentieth-floor terrace, on a walkway across a tall bridge, or out on some scenic observation deck.

Inching toward the edge of the roof, Phil said:

> God, what do You want us to learn from phobias?
> Fearing things that may be dangerous,
> Like perilous heights and poisonous snakes
> Is understandable.
> But when you make some of us
> Scared out of our wits
> Over the number 13
> Or strangers,
> That's striking fear into our hearts,
> It seems, for no earthly purpose.

To which God replied, "You figure it out."

Many people who have prayed, and have thought that they had prayed fervently and honestly, have eventually pooh-poohed prayer as being ineffectual, if not downright hokum. In their estimation, "God didn't listen."

Strange, isn't it? In a conversational situation when one person is speaking to another, the listener is not required to constantly say, "Uh-huh . . . I see . . . oh yes, I hear you . . . uh-huh." The listener can be quite attentive—and silent. Yet people seem to demand a definitive response from God every time they talk to Him. People expect a response, if not in words, in strong and obvious and, from the pray-ers' perspective, a positive action.

Scientists have told us over and over again that a human being possesses millions upon millions of brain cells he never uses. Not because he *can't* use them. He either hasn't had the occasion to use them or has chosen not to use them. So when God tells us, "You figure it out," God is not being sarcastic. He is simply urging us to use a small percentage of those myriad brain cells that may end up accompanying us to the grave unused.

Phil's surplus brain cells wrestled with the irrational phobia issue for a while. Then Phil had to move on to the privets. To prune them. And to the holly. To shape it. And then to the pansies. To nip them. Which got him to thinking, not about phobias, but about regeneration.

> I nip off the once glorious, now fading flowers
> And in a few days the purged plant
> Renews itself with even more glorious blossoms
> And in greater number, too.
> Now, what would it be like, God,
> If I lopped away from my life
> Some of the tired old passions I hang on to?
> Would I be any different or better
> Without my long-standing attachments
> To ceramic frogs and the New York Giants,
> Restaurant matchbooks and *Gourmet Magazines,*
> License plates and show albums and *Playbills?*
> Having rid myself of these former joys,
> Would I find new and even more flaming passions

Or would a new and less-cluttered me
Look at life quite differently?

When God has said, "You figure it out," to people, some of them
have taken off for deserts and caves and other spots of mystical seclu-
sion. May I suggest that the seven-tenths of an acre or so that one
considers one's suburban digs can be just as productive a "figuring it
out" place?

Think of all the mindless—and I use that word not as a synonym for
"dumb" but as a synonym for "no thinking required"—activities you
perform around the house, almost robotic activities, during which time
you can wrestle with the questions you and God have asked yourselves
and never quite got around to answering. Activities like raking leaves
and shoveling snow, mowing the lawn and digging up dandelions, paint-
ing the house and washing the car give you that precious opportunity.
City life, apartment life, even brownstone life, just can't provide you
with those priceless monotonous moments for meditation.

And that meditation, as I have mentioned before and shall mention
again, need not deal with subjects that haunt men's souls or glands. For
example, there's an object, a garden vegetable actually, that I have
taken—or, rather, that has taken me—from passing interest to obsessive
passion. And I'm not alone in this suburban madness. There are hundreds, perhaps thousands of others who share my uncontrollable ardor
for this humble veggie.

Let me, neighbors—which, of course, includes You—make a clean
breast of it. Let me confess to this all-consuming passion. And, as I've
just said, the passion's not mine alone. It doesn't matter whether or not
we have a genetic knack for gardening, whether we have been blessed
with a pair of those cliché thumbs or not. Whatever our background
and bent, we have this unrequitable love affair with . . . the tomato.
We suburban men (do women feel the same way about the tomato that
we do, God?) are compelled to grow it, stake it, nurture it, harvest it,
flaunt it.

Anybody can see it for himself. A drive through any suburban town
will drive it home. Whether one's property stretches for acres or
whether one's domain is a humble plot, there'll be a tomato plant or a
dozen growing on it. Just how did this mania come about?

Is there some geographical explanation?

Well, the tomato is a well-traveled vegetable. Its origin, curiously enough, is not the Old World but the New: Mexico and Peru. The tomato eventually arrived in Europe, courtesy of the Spanish, who managed to stuff a few plants in their bags of pillaged South American gold. Yet, even on the supposedly with-it Continent, the tomato remained merely an ornamental plant until the sixteenth century. Only then did some anonymous pioneer health faddist toss a tomato into a salad. And only in the past century, back here in the Americas, specifically the U.S. of A., did the tomato become the legendary staple that it is.

Well, neighbors, that bit of geographical history doesn't give us any clues as to why we suburban males are now so tomato-crazed. The answer doesn't lie with Rand-McNally. Maybe it rests—pardon me, Father—with Freud.

We males, especially we suburban males, are the archetypical overachievers. ("Overachiever" is not synonymous with "workaholic," although they may share some attributes.) We climb the slipperiest of corporate ladders, professing to love every minute of the climb. We battle indefatigably in every sport imaginable, polite or brutal. We seek competitive vents at every turn—even during those few hours we spend at home. Well, then, what better at-home vent for our competitiveness than to grow *more* tomatoes, *plumper* tomatoes, *juicier* tomatoes than our neighbor? What indeed! We are driven by this desire to prove to our neighbor undeniably, incontrovertibly that we have a better sense of humus than he does.

And the agronomists, those canny creatures of Yours, God, recognize this facet/flaw of our personality. They recognize it and exploit it. Look at what seedmen, shamelessly playing to our maleness, call the various varieties of tomatoes. There is Big Boy and there is Better Boy. There are Ultra Boy, Wonder Boy and Golden Boy. Why, there's even a variety called Vigor Boy—and should a suburban cultivator yearn for something even manlier, more Nautilesque, than those offerings, he can actually grow up to grow He Man tomatoes.

Satisfying? Gratifying? To be sure, but the road to He-Manhood is fraught with perils. Perils that give us fitful nights, perils that we call nematodes and verticillium wilt, fusarium and race, and that cruelly devastating tobacco mosaic virus. With all these blights ready to attack our precious plants, is it any wonder that we are growing bald—at least I am—with worry? Is it any wonder that we take the wildest, most expensive precautions with our crop? Anyone agri-motoring through the burbs will find us spraying and powdering our precious Ramapos,

Rushmores, and Royal Chicos, painstakingly laboring to deter the potential ravages of the aforementioned plagues.

But since I am confessing, Friend and neighbors, to this fixation, I may as well make a totally spanking immaculately clean breast of it. I must even own up to the rather new practice, a ritual of recent vintage that we pomme d'amourists have taken up. It happens early in the growing season, and the ritual provides a clear, if frightening, example of just how competitive we tomato growers really are.

As soon as the first tomato blossoms burst into golden loveliness, we are out there spraying those early flowers with a *hormone fixative*. Yes, there is such a thing, a marvelous chemical we use to ensure that the first tomato blossoms, which if left to Mother Nature would drop off fruitlessly, will indeed stay on the vine and bear fruit. And right away. In fact, these hormonally fixed blossoms will turn into tomatoes so fast that my neighbors will be amazed, shocked and writhing with envy to see that I have red ripe tomatoes weeks before they have even any green ones. Now, how important is this advantage? What does it do for my ego? That's the reason for this confession, neighbors. It means everything to me.

And should it, really? Must I be that competitive, that passionate? Isn't gardening, according to *my* definition, a time for meditation, not one-upmanship?

Karel Čapek may not have thought so. The dramatist who gave us the robot gave some consideration to humans as well. And perhaps in his native Czechoslovakia Čapek grew tomatoes too. He certainly understood us tomato gardeners, for Čapek wrote, "Let no one think that real gardening is a bucolic and meditative occupation; it is an insatiable passion, like everything else to which a man gives his heart."

WEDNESDAY NIGHT

Frzzbk, Blang, Brring, Skritch Skritch,
Hrgh Hrgh

Sounds are affirmations of life. Sounds at night tell us there is life after sleep. And during sleep. To interrupt our sleep.

Janice and Phil, but especially Janice, who has more difficulty falling asleep than Phil does, appreciate the white-sound noise of the dishwasher. The dishwasher is turned on nightly just before the lights are turned out. And although the dishwasher is in the kitchen, as it doggone well ought to be, rooms away from Janice and Phil's bedroom, the droning of its motor, the programmed splash of its wash cycle, and the rhythmic clink of an improperly seated glass, tend to wash away the day for Janice and lull her to sleep.

But there is a counternoise to the pleasant dishwasher sound that can negate all of its tranquilizing benefits. If the sound of the dishwasher is a restful white sound, the noises emanating from the neighbor's electronic bug killer must be considered, well, sort of a blazing orange. And just as startling as the color itself. When a neighbor has such a device attached to a post or the wall in the back of the house, it's virtually impossible for anyone in the neighborhood to sleep with the window open. Those periodic frzzbks and grzzls throughout an August night will roust even as deep a sleeper as Phil.

Then there are the sounds of the nocturnal beasties. Up in the attic a pesky squirrel is skittering about. The clever little rodent—and let no man ever forget that the cute squirrel is in fact a rodent!—has managed to squeeze through a roof vent and finds jumping from beam to beam a welcome, and safer, diversion than leaping from tree limb to tree limb. But how does one keep the vent open and the squirrel out? That gnawing (which is just what the squirrel is doing) question perplexes a momentarily roused Phil. But he is further roused, into a sitting position, by . . .

. . . Blang! The darling but voracious bane of suburbia produces his wee-hour clatter as once again the lid is pried off the garbage can and it topples, scattering its contents over the driveway. B.J. had placed two sizable logs on top of the can to make the raccoon's foray more difficult. More difficult, perhaps, but certainly not impossible.

These night sounds, although aggravating, aren't really frightening. What's frightening is the sound of the telephone ringing at 1 A.M. It can't be, just can't be, good news at that hour. (Granny has often told her grandchildren—just as she had told her own children—as they went out at night, ". . . and remember, nothing good has ever happened after eleven.") A call after midnight can only mean trouble, and Janice swallows hard when she hears the operator say, "Collect call from Phil. Will you accept the charges?"

"Yes, yes, yes," says Janice to the operator—and to her sleeping husband (who hasn't even heard the ring), "Wake up, wake up, Phil . . . it's Junior." Janice's summons is accompanied by a less-than-gentle poke in her husband's gently and rhythmically heaving chest.

"Wha? Wha?" gurgles Senior as he sits up beside his frantic wife, who hears a rather cheery voice on the other end of the phone say, "Hi, Mom. How's it going?"

"How's it going?" Janice repeats, her interrogative squeal piercing the bedroom darkness. This time the pique is mixed with parental concern. "How are you? What's wrong, Phil? What's happened?"

"Nothing wrong. Nothing's happened."

"Then, why are you calling at . . . at . . ."—Janice squints at the green light of the bedside clock—". . . at one fourteen at night?"

"Oh, sorry, yeah. I didn't realize it was *that* time. I knew it was kinda late, but not *that* late. It's just that tomorrow is the last day . . . well, it's tomorrow already, heh heh heh, so today is the last day to reserve a room off campus for next semester—and I wanted to clear it with you guys, because it'll be about four hundred dollars more than living *on* campus."

"Off campus?" Janice repeats, not out of confusion or ignorance but just to slow her son's speech up.

Phil the Father, unable to hear his son's part of the conversation, asks his wife, "What's he doing off campus at this hour of the night on a week night?"

"Nothing," snaps Janice. "He's not off campus . . . he wants to *move* off campus."

"Tonight?"

"No," says Janice out of the side of her mouth to her husband. Out of the other side she says to her son, "What prompted all this, Phil?"

"Well, there's this terrific house . . . like a boarding house . . . that's just been assigned to the Arts Department to house kids who are interested in the arts, which I am, and I got a chance to get in . . . and there's this neat kid from West Virginia named Lee who'd move in with me and . . ."

"And you waited till now . . . till . . . one sixteen tonight . . . this morning . . . to call and ask us?"

"Look, Mom, I got so much to think about . . . c'mon, I'm carryin' five courses . . . I forgot. So I forgot. Is that such a big deal? And I said I'm sorry . . . I mean, one o'clock is late for you guys, but it's not late for us."

After another ten minutes of conversation, more out of relief at the non-life-threatening nature of the call than belief that an off-campus living experience would be beneficial to their son, Janice and Phil agree to Phil, Junior's, request. The call finally concluded, the noncrisis at last resolved, husband and wife now speak a few monosyllables at one another. The first monosyllables come from Janet:

"What a dope."

"He's a kid."

"Yes, but . . ."

"He's fine."

"He's too young to . . ."

"Just fine."

"You think so?"

"Sure."

"Well, I don't know."

"Go to sleep."

"How can I sleep?"

"*I* can sleep."

"That's for sure."

"Good night."

"Good night."

And those are the last words Janice and Phil speak to one another this night. To one another, but not to God. Each in her/his own way, each in her/his own idiom, each on her/his own pillow, tells God how she/he feels about the call from her/his son at college.

Janice says:

> He *will* grow up, I suppose,
> With Your guidance and grace.
> But as he does, Good God,
> Could you give me some hints
> That it's happening?
> His life is as disorganized
> As his room has always been.
> His decisions always seem to be
> Spur-of-the-moment ones.
> Yet the thing that bothers me most
> Is that he's always so upbeat about *every*-thing.
> He sure didn't get that bubbliness
> From his father or mother.
> It's You, isn't it?
> He got it from You.

And Phil, with his head buried in his pillow, says to God:

> Help him, won't You, Father,
> Through these years of trial and error?
> And help Janice, too, to understand
> That maturing may take her son
> More time than it takes others,
> More time than she might want to give it.
> Oh, I believe You'll see
> That Phil grows up
> Eventually,
> But tell me, God,
> Is Lee

    A he
    Or a she?

This is followed by that most reliable of night sounds, the baritone hrgh hrgh of Phil's snoring.

THURSDAY MORNING

Permanent Relationships

To those who have searched for God—in the suburbs and beyond—and have found their searching to be futile, I have a suggestion. There's one place you may have overlooked. Oh, you've looked everywhere, you say? Where else can you possibly look? What else can you conceivably do to find God?

Try this. *Stick your head in a hair drier.*

About a decade ago I began having my hair done by my wife's hairdresser. This wasn't so much a result of any unisexual enlightenment on my part but, rather, out of frustration at barbers who, despite the fact that my hair was thinning rather rapidly, sheared me in such a fashion as to highlight my scalp instead of hiding it. Perhaps the masterful Andrew, who had frosted and curled and permed my wife so well through the years, could work similar magic on me.

Whether he has succeeded or not is open to debate. But his shop has most assuredly—and serendipitously—succeeded in transforming many of his other patrons, in a matter of minutes, from anxious, self-interested souls into some of the community's most solicitous and nice-to-be-with individuals.

It works like this: A woman comes into Andrew's, frowning, frazzled and fifteen minutes late for her appointment. (Yes, it's a woman. Although a few men have joined me as patrons of Andrew's hair salon, the establishment is still primarily a women's domain.) The customer announces her reason for frowning, for being frazzled, and for being fifteen minutes late. She announces it to the entire assemblage. The assemblage is two operators, a manicurist, a shampooer, and five women in various stages of coiffeurial renewal. The customer's reason for being emotionally as well as physically disheveled is a rather minor household calamity, but that mini-calamity has given her a topic for hair-salon conversation.

And converse she does. Elaborating all the while on the problem to any of the assemblage who care to listen, Frowning and Frazzled has her hair washed and set and is sent to the drier. Now the transformation begins.

I have seen it with my own eyes—as I look into Frowning and Frazzled's eyes. A liquid serenity comes over them. It's not a glaze; it's a transparent sheen. As the heat dries her hair, the bugged and bothered woman seems to be warming too—warming to her surroundings and the people in the shop(pe). She's taking notice of them. Her thoughts are shifting from self to others.

Of all the tranquilizers, physical and psychic, written and talked about today, has anyone explored the possibility of tranquilizing someone by heating the head? Could be something to it. I'm not sure. But I *am* sure that a hair drier is a direct connection to God. Although Once Frowning and Frazzled's lips aren't moving, you can almost hear her saying to God:

C'mon, I'm not a phone slammer,
So why did I bang it down on Jim
When he called to tell me he had invited
His cousin and her family for the weekend?
You know I'm not a phone slammer,
I know I'm not a phone slammer,
And I'll call Jim at the office
And tell him I'm not a phone slammer.
No big deal, putting up
Jim's cousin and the kids
For the weekend.

Hmmmm . . . the manicurist's eyes look gray.
Has she been having trouble sleeping?
Is something bothering her?

Hmmmm . . . isn't Andrew going off to St. Maarten next week?
I better tell him about
That marvelous restaurant on the French side.

Hmmmm . . . Helen's lost a lot of weight.
I must tell her
How good she looks.

Hmmmm. . . .

It is quite conceivable that silent cerebral chats with the Creator are going on in every one of the hair driers in use. Consider what happens when the women slide out from beneath the driers. No longer are they antsy or edgy, bothered or just plain mad. Their innate compassionate natures have taken over once again. Now the women are tenderly commiserating with and counseling the manicurist, whose boyfriend, it is revealed, has lost his job. They clue Andrew in on restaurants not only in St. Maarten, but since he's such a restaurant lover and traveler, on new eating spots in Washington, Palm Beach and the upper West Side. And the women all rave about Helen's new trimmed-down figure: "A knock-out," "Wow, do you look good!" "How did you do it, Helen, can you tell me your secret?"

To those people who like to think of beauty parlors as dens of gossip and snideness, I suggest suspending those beliefs until they research the hair drier / God connection for themselves. I think they'll be surprised. And tranquilized. And if they're open to it, transformed, too.

One more observation on time spent at the hairdresser's, although this note might more accurately appear under "Saturday Morning," rather than "Thursday Morning," since that's when I ordinarily visit Andrew's: there is no better place for a man to learn to be comfortable with women than at the hairdresser's.

No matter how much a man may profess to empathize with a woman's feelings and needs, it is almost impossible for him to reflect them accurately. That's because a man is seldom alone in the company of women when those feelings are being openly discussed. But after just a few appointments at Andrew's, I felt totally at ease joining in discussions on sexual harassment at the office, premenstrual syndrome and face-lifts. I even found myself sharing my own concerns about losing hair and gaining weight, a couple of subjects I have never found it easy to talk about, even in the company of male friends.

Candor and comfort and yet another reminder from God (via hair drier) that our humanity is meant to be shared—these are a few of the perks-of-the-spirit that go with regular visits to your hairdresser.

THURSDAY AFTERNOON

Chipped off the Old Block

Parents Day in the Ames school system has been a tradition for generations. Many of the Ames Junior High teachers, tenure being the felicitous institution it is, eagerly greet parents whom they used to teach years ago, when those parents were youngsters.

As for those parents, most of them truly enjoy these back-to-school rituals. There is something pleasantly, nostalgically silly about sitting in a cramped classroom seat. Then there's the opportunity presented to review each teacher's mini-presentation of his or her subject. The parent can then grade the teacher on the teacher's ability to make the subject vital and exciting to the little heir being taught.

Phil, having attended most of the Parents Days when firstborn Phil was a student, having been as faithful as business travel would allow while Jennifer has been in school, is now finding going to Parents Day for B.J. something of a drag. Phil is finally déjà-vuing and "So what's new-ing" at explanations of how Latin is important in understanding English vocabulary and syntax, and why parental support is needed for the music programs so that the chorus and the band can travel to perform and compete and how the teachers are happy to have a private parent conference anytime a mother or a father would care to discuss a child's progress or lack thereof.

But Phil suppresses and sublimates. Tradition and love and support of his youngest child compel him to join Janice for this year's Parents

Day program, which begins, as do all Parents Day programs, with greetings from the principal. As the lanky, angular, and obviously toupeed principal steps to the podium, Phil catches himself as he is about to whisper something to Janice, and he whispers to God instead:

> Watch me today, God, like Your proverbial hawk,
> And stifle any inclination I might have to mock.

Stereotypes and clichés are a great temptation for Phil. He has an insatiable itch to satirize. He is a born mimic, and somewhat of a cynic, so Phil must constantly be on guard lest one of his offhand remarks be interpreted as malicious, not hilarious. And especially here, now, at Parents Day. The event can be a satirist's delight.

Throughout the afternoon, Phil will learn that his wit, well intentioned in the main, may be somewhat of a genetic burden. As the father introduces himself to his son's many teachers, Phil hears synopses of B.J.'s performance in the classroom such as "He has such a keen mind . . . and tongue to match" and "B.J. certainly *does* speak his mind" and "What a delightful, generally speaking, sense of humor your son has" and "Bit of a cutup, doncha know."

This latter observation comes from B.J.'s European-history teacher, a young Englishman who is experiencing some difficulty adjusting to America's looser and louder classroom style. Once more, as Phil is about to hang a cutesy Anglo appellation on the teacher, he catches himself and repeats:

> Watch me today, God, like Your proverbial hawk,
> And stifle any inclination I might have to mock.

This particular yen to be clever having been nipped in the barb, Phil is confronted next with a situation that requires him not merely to hold his tongue, but bite it. The imposing Miss Talbot is assistant principal, and one of her duties is to encourage and promote discipline at AJH. In this role Miss Talbot and B.J. have, on numerous occasions (sorry, but the trite and abused expression seems most appropriate here) *interfaced.*

Although Phil had not intended to visit with Miss Talbot, saw no reason to, the disciplinarian seeks him out. She stops Phil in the corridor and immediately puts him on the defensive. "Good afternoon. I am Miss Talbot. Might we have a word?" Who, thinks Phil, introduces herself as Miss these days? Doesn't the woman have a first name? And what's with the "Might we have a word"? Phil, stifling his natural inclination to answer, "Indeedy-do we might," replies instead, "Certainly."

Miss Talbot, leading Phil ("Where's Janice when I need her?") into her office ("It figures . . . it figures, she sits in a wing chair!") announces, "A disciplinary update on your son, if you will." Throughout the ten-minute run-through of B.J.'s escapades of the past semester, Miss Talbot never refers to B.J. by his initials. Nor by his name. ("Talbot's the name, laying guilt's the game.") She repeatedly speaks of B.J. as "your son."

As ticked off by the disciplinary officer, some of B.J.'s practical jokes *have* unarguably, even by his father, been disruptive and dumb. But Phil admits to himself, in a semiperverse internalized display of paternal pride, that some of B.J.'s gags have been inspired.

Putting a Band-Aid on his forehead and asking the teacher if he could be excused from class because he had a splitting headache was a recent B.J. prank in the finest Abbott and Costello tradition. And when asked by his English teacher to use the word "pigment" in a sentence, B.J. promptly shot back, "I understood what the horse said, but I didn't know what the pigment." For this the kid should have been sent to Miss Talbot's office?

No way—in Phil's estimation. But that isn't Phil's biggest problem with Miss Talbot. It's her amateur psychoanalyzing. ("Does she have a couch in here somewhere, maybe tucked away behind the wing chair? Can you believe it? A wing chair? In a school office?") When the assistant principal says, "Your son's opting to resort to comedy on a continuing basis may be a compensatory action for some heretofore unidentified character flaw," Phil feels his neck muscles tighten. And when she begins to pontificate, in how-to book language, that "growing up means growing out of certain habits," Phil stands up and says, "Miss Talbot . . . excuse me . . . what is your first name?"

"Why . . . eh . . . it's . . . it's Veronica."

"Well now, Veronica, I will *indeed* take your comments to heart. And I'll take them to B.J., too, heh heh. And I shall think about your remarks . . . and your . . . your analysis of my son, and from time to time, you can say to yourself . . . Phil . . . that's *my* first name . . . you can say Phil is thinking about what I said . . . and I'll be saying . . . Veronica said some mighty provocative things . . . and we'll sort of be on the same . . . heh heh . . . wavelength. I thank you . . . *indeed* I do . . . and remember, Phil will be thinking about what you . . . what Veronica said."

Although Phil's parting words (and he parts, he parts very quickly) to Miss Veronica Talbot are facetious and rash and a bit dopey, the business of remembering a person from time to time, especially a person who has been somewhat unpleasant to you, has merit.

Some of us, although God felt we were important enough to be created, still feel we must constantly give testimony of our importance to others. It may be an importance we feel we have because of our work role, as in Miss Talbot's case, or our social role, or in flaunting a particular skill we might have. These persistent affirmations of importance can make the speaker seem pompous, the spoken-to seem *un*-important or, as is most frequently the case, both. Yet, every single day, we run into these "I'm important" posturers. And every so often we have to fight the inclination to be an "I'm important" posturer ourselves.

Phil's farewell statement to Veronica Talbot, sarcastic though it was, presents a possible way to help self-important people, certainly a better way than telling them outright, "Get off it . . . you're not really all that important." By letting the person know that, yes, she *is* important and you'll be thinking about her (and her importance), the person who once had to rely on her skills as a disciplinarian, for example, to manifest her imagined importance, may now have received enough satisfaction knowing that she honest and truly has made an impression on someone. Someone is thinking about her. And that alone may be enough to have her temper any further displays of self-importance.

Consider the expression "all wrapped up in oneself." Now imagine what a boost to one's ego it would be if that person could know that you and your thoughts would be "wrapped up" in him and her every so often. It need not be someone close or beloved. No, a passing acquaintance, a sometime associate, a neighbor, an assistant principal. Much the same way God is "wrapped up" in all of us—all the time. We could elevate someone's life by wrapping our thoughts around that person once in a while. A thought. Just a thought.

And one final plus of a back-to-school experience for a parent. It can have a lovely and nostalgic "what might have been" effect. On the other hand, it can also have a sad and wrenching "what might have been" effect. That "might have been" can apply, under differing circumstances, to the children one is back-to-schooling for, or to oneself.

Janice listens to the school orchestra saw and squeal away. The sounds are faintly familiar. Strauss perhaps. Janice remembers how everyone thought Phil, Junior, would have a legendary musical career. But Phil, who played both violin and piano extraordinarily well in junior high, discovered the guitar and electricity and Jimi Hendrix in high school. What might have been a classical music vocation became an ear-piercing weekend avocation. And as for Phil's swimming prowess and his medals and championships and all-county honors, the only swimming he's done at college has been skinny-dipping at three in the morning in Lake Gnatz.

Jennifer might have been the best French student in high school, could have spent this year as an exchange student in Paris, but chose to stay stateside and run for secretary of her class instead. She campaigned hard and won, being gifted (is it a gift?) with more of a killer instinct than her mom has. Yet, Janice muses as she breathes in the musty memory-jogging smell of chalk dust, what an experience a year in France would have been for Jen.

As for B.J., it's a little too soon for "what might have beens." At twelve, B.J. still has a world of "might be's" ahead of him.

Phil's reminiscing at Parents Day goes back farther than Janice's reminiscing. Farther by about thirty years. Phil remembers when he was in the seventh grade himself, the way B.J. is now, and how he was positively crazy about a girl with the softest hair he had ever felt, or, as he imagines, has ever felt since. Jeannie was the girl's name and she rode the same school bus that Phil did. Jeannie was Phil's goddess. He fantasized writing her someday when he mustered up enough nerve, addressing the girl as "Dear Dea Mea." If there are such things as fantasizer prodigies, Phil was one.

On the ride to and from school, Phil would try to get to sit with his Jeannie and make small talk with his Jeannie until . . . until the day Jeannie told Phil she had received a U card in English. U stood for Unsatisfactory, and those cards went out in midterm to inform parents that their kids better shape up or risk failing the subject.

A U card? And in English? *His* Jeannie? *His* goddess? Could this lovely thing with the soft hair, this *dea mea* he was wild about, be . . . be . . . dumb?

Phil never sat on the bus with, or talked to, Jeannie again.

The regret not only remains, but it seems to come back stronger and more rueful whenever it's jogged to Phil's consciousness by something like a Parents Day. How could this intelligent kid, this fantasizer prodigy, even at twelve or thirteen, ever have been such a snobby jerk as to feel that a girl, even the most beautiful girl in the world, would be unworthy of him if she got a U card in English? Arrrggh! (Nostalgic regrets are sometimes so painful they are accompanied by hideous back-of-the-throat sounds.) Arrrggh! If he hadn't been such a dope, what kind of relationship might he have had with Jeannie? Would they have grown up as childhood sweethearts? College sweethearts? (But what kind of college could Jeannie have gotten into with *her* marks?) Arrrggh! Might they have married? Where's Jeannie today? Is her hair still wondrously soft?

"What might have beens," contrary to one opinion, are not the fruit-less mental meanderings of sorry folk riveted to the past. "What might have beens" stretch our imagination, rekindle significant memories and, most important, let us intelligently assess "what actually is." That assessment can lead us to grateful rejoicing about our present station or a midlife correction of one kind or another. Either way, it's a positive end result of harking back and imagining "what might have been."

Veronica Talbot, bless her aphoristic soul, might have put it this way: "To grow wiser, never grow away from old memories." To which Phil, most likely, would have said, "Gee, thanks, Veronica. Really, thanks. I'll remember that. And I'll remember that *you* are the one who told me that . grow wiser . . . never grow away . . . nice construction. Thanks. Thanks a lot."

THURSDAY NIGHT

TV Prayers

November, according to the television rating service A. C. Nielsen, is the most stable viewing month. Here, then, are some eye-opening statistics for November 1985. American women between the ages of eighteen and thirty-four had *their* eyes open in front of a TV set for thirty-two hours and twenty-one minutes a week . . . *a week,* during that very typical month. American men were glued to the tube for twenty-six hours and three minutes a week. So that means that, depending on our own individual priorities, there is the distinct possibility that some of us spend more time with Bill Cosby, Jane Pauley and John Madden than we do with our own family during the course of a week. Oh, but that's not to imply that television is an evil. Not at all. Television can be a wonderful escape; it can also be a marvelous restorative.

Yet in all our viewing there are also stretches of blah. Yes, there are many lulls, many empty moments, many commercials and station breaks and opportunities.

Opportunities?

Yes, *extraordinary* opportunities.

For what? Running off to the bathroom? To the refrigerator?

Sure, but I wouldn't call those opportunities extraordinary. I mean extraordinary in the sense that there is nothing during the course of the week that gives us the chance to talk to God the way our weekly TV viewing does.

You see, not only does television give us the time—but then again, as we've seen, other activities can do that as well—to chat with the Creator in a casual, colloquial way, but TV can also provide us with much of the subject matter of those conversations and, if not the actual topics themselves, certainly a host of divine icebreakers, ways to ease into our brief but, let's hope, frequent and helpful chats with God.

TV gives us more such opportunities than any activity imaginable. For example, after you've either smiled or shuddered at ladies squeezing a roll of toilet paper for the hundred-and-umpteenth time, you are quite amenable to swapping thirty seconds with Mr. Whipple for thirty seconds with God. In fact, that can be the most striking example of going from the ridiculous to the sublime in the history of the expression.

Critics of television say it's a mindless medium, a hypnotic thing in front of which people sit to flee from reality. Frank Lloyd Wright called television "chewing gum for the eyes." Be it mindless or mesmerizing or even occasionally magnificent entertainment, television does present us with this superb and transcendental opportunity.

Imagine being able to sit in your TV room (and the suburban home has up to three, and sometimes more, TV rooms), take a cue from the show you're watching and use that cue to talk to God either at that very moment or during the commercial clutter that is inevitably part of the show.

If we could get into the habit of daytime or prime-time or any-time praying, imagine the hundreds of hundreds of conversations we all could have with God week after thirty-two-hour-and-twenty-one-minute viewing week.

Our occasions for this channeled communication with the Creator can begin as early as seven in the morning, when we stumble our way into the kitchen, turn on both Mr. Coffee and "The Today Show" and say to God:

> The familiar faces greet me once again,
> Reassuring me that all's well with the world,
> Although the bombings and disasters they show
> Should lead me to believe otherwise.
> Why am I not frightened?
> Why don't I feel threatened
> As I waken to war
> And mayhem and murder?

Is it because of the familiar faces
Who are giving me the news—
Or is it because of my
Fragile faith in You?

Yes, those faces on the tube in the morning may be familiar. But they may not be all that comforting. In fact, some of those faces may have just the opposite effect—they may be *dis*-comforting. That's especially true when a face leads to a Godchat that brings to the surface a dimension of your character that you're not all that wild about. For instance, the ubiquitous weather forecaster has just gone through his high-pressure, low-pressure spiel, and you say to God:

He smiles through sleet and snow;
He grins when records of discomfort are broken.
Has that smile of his been frozen in place
By some prolonged cold spell this past winter?
But why am I bothered by this happy forecaster?
Is it that I don't believe his happiness is real?
Or is it that *I* fall short of
Flashing contentment,
Showing satisfaction,
Preferring to wear a stony, uncaring stare
Than a smile that says,
"I'm with you . . . I understand."

Teach me, God, to be more like
That man in front of the satellite weather photo,
Who can sense scientifically
What I *should* sense spiritually;
Namely, that things will always get better.
Amen.

There you are in the kitchen, you haven't even managed to wrestle the English muffin out of the toaster yet (careful, don't use a fork . . . use something wooden), and you've already found a couple of television cues to get you into early-morning touch with God. But maybe you've had enough news, weather and sports and you decide to switch to a morning exercise program. There it is. The rock music. The rock-hard body of the video instructor. You listen and watch for a while and say:

I can't imagine *my* body ever stretching
Into the positions she's suggesting,
Yet *You're* suggesting,
If I'm hearing You right,
That I stretch my *conscience*
In ways that seem impossible too.
You're telling this to me,
Me, who find it less of a struggle
To touch my toes
Than to touch someone's heart.
Well, let me chew on it,
Stew over it,
And, as You're hearing now,
Pray about it,
And then,
Who knows, God,
Who knows?

As that impromptu prayer, which is really more of a response, shows, a conversation with God need not be conclusive. The talk can be nothing more than the exposition of a feeling or a doubt, a snippet of joy or a pang of anxiety. Or it can be an off-the-wall thought that you never would have conceived your rather conservative and conventional mind ever coming up with. You may be watching "Wheel of Fortune" (can you believe it?—one in every six women in America do!) or "Jeopardy" or "The Price Is Right" or any game show and comment to God:

She jumps up and down
Hugging the emcee
Yelping her thanks
For the money and the drier
And the weekend in Paris.
All the game-show winners, it seems,
Express their delight
With howls and squeals and shrieks.
I wonder, Almighty Father,
Has anyone entered eternity
Letting out a wild whoop of joy?
If not, Lord,
And if You don't think it unseemly,

> Might I be the first?
> Amen.

Hugging emcees, a Buscaglia imperative perhaps, can lead to thoughts of eternal joy. Maybe even protracted earthly joy. The talk-show kiss, on the other hand (or other cheek) may lead to this supplication:

> They always seem to kiss,
> The host and his guests,
> As they greet one another
> Prior to their chat.
> Is this peck,
> This salutatory kiss,
> Out of affection
> Or just for effect?
> Yet why should I be bothered
> By this display of caring,
> And whether the kiss is
> For real or for show?
> What harm would it do,
> Dear God, I ask you,
> If the whole human race
> Were more kissy-face?

A Johnny Carson smooch on Susie Starlet's cheek may seem, to some, a strange or an inappropriate segue into a conversation with God. But it's not. There is no life lead-in that I can think of that's too strange or mundane, too earthy or too trivial, for a quick communication with the Creator. Yes, some TV offerings may evoke a more soul-searching reaction/prayer than other TV fare. The afternoon soaps, for example, can elicit this:

> The Monday through Friday agonies
> All those characters suffer
> Fade with the credits
> (At least for me they do).
> I can step back, step away,
> Step out of the house
> And forget soapsorrows for a time.
> But for those who, through weakness or illness,

> Are bound to their box of afternoon misery,
> Grant them the insight to see that all
> That TV misery has been magnified
> For drama's sake,
> But for *their* sake there is always
> Your boundless love and compassion.
> Amen.

Perhaps the only television enthusiasts who can match a soap lover's enthusiasm in eyeball-riveting devotion are the sports fans. I am one. I will watch just about anything on television in which one team or a person ends up winning and a team or a person ends up losing.

Well, *almost* anything.

I draw the line at "Family Feud."

But I'm wild about baseball. I enjoy basketball games, at least the last five minutes of them. And I can't wait for the leaves to start turning. That's when I am able to turn the channel selector madly and find two, three or four football games being televised simultaneously.

This used to be a weekend passion of mine. Like almost all passions, this one I share with millions of others demanded to be extended, prolonged, kept flaming as long as possible. ABC has allowed us to do that. "Monday Night Football" also allows us many, many moments during each telecast when we can speak with God:

> I watched two on Saturday,
> Parts of three on Sunday
> And here I am Monday night,
> Hoping for a high-scoring game,
> Rather than a defensive struggle.
> What does that say about me,
> All-Knowing Father?
> That I am never bored
> Watching twenty-two men collide
> Every thirty seconds or so?
> Does it mean I am
> Incorrigibly aggressive,
> Need constant excitement,
> Crave action on demand?
> Remind me, God,
> Every so often,

> To be as passionate
> About running to eternity
> As I tend to be
> About watching a fullback
> Run to daylight.
> Amen.

And try to imagine all the times we have grinned and borne—but not all that well—the interminable time-outs during football games. How interminable? Not as interminable to us at home as to those at the stadium. People at the game must watch the players mill about for ninety seconds. We at home can watch Mr. Goodwrench on the tube and talk to God alongside us.

> Neither team called time out;
> The referee did,
> So that the network could get in
> Some more commercials.
> Did You ever think, God Almighty,
> To call a commercial time-out on life?
> I mean, stop everything
> For ninety seconds or so—
> Stop work,
> Stop play,
> Stop war.
> And get in three hard-hitting messages
> Of Your own,
> Say, on the dignity of work,
> The joy of play,
> And the absurdity of war?

As I've mentioned, football is not my only televised sports passion. Every sport that's televised holds a fascination for me, even shows—and perhaps especially those shows—that serve up a little of this and a little of that, a sports smorgasbord, as it were, which gives me the occasion to say to God:

> Wrist wrestling, motocross,
> Drag racing, barrel jumping—
> What is it about the universal us
> That demands we compete?

Not only compete,
But sit bug-eyed, even breathless,
Watching our brothers and sisters
In some sort of contrived
Head-to-head or
Toe-to-toe confrontation?
Would that we could work up
The same healthy fervor
For justice and freedom
That we work up for bowl games.
Just a thought,
Just a wish,
During this lull in the action,
Offered up and sent
From my bench to Yours.
Amen.

Then there's the case of the malfunctioning set. Mitsubishi's and Panasonic's promises notwithstanding, sometimes TV sets don't work perfectly. What happens when a particular channel's reception isn't all that terrific? Well, it's given me the opportunity to say:

Some channels come in fuzzier than others.
So do some of my values.
I can be crystal clear on Tyranny and War
And rather blurry on The Expedient Lie.
Sharpen *my* focus, I pray, God,
That I may see the potential harm
In my little exaggerations.
Grace me with a clearer picture
Of exactly what's right;
Yes, sharpen *my* focus,
And if You don't mind my asking,
Can You do something about
Channel 9, too?
Amen.

Then there are the specific things that go wrong, things like the vertical and the horizontal holds malfunctioning. C'mon, you might say, how can vertical and horizontal problems be springboards for prayer? Well, why not? Why, when the vertical hold begins to distort the picture, can't someone be moved to say:

Why are all the bodies curving,
All the letters rippling
Across the screen and off?
Is it a sudden shortage of juice
Or a general winding down
Of the whole old mechanism?
A winding down?
A winding down?
Dear God, Compassionate God,
Even if it be Your will
That *I* wind down,
Rather than drop off,
In the winding
May I always have
Just enough strength
To extol the wonders of You
As reflected in the wonders of us.
Amen.

It could be that I have had more television problems than the normal consumer. And the problems aren't always the same. It might be the vertical hold—or it might be the horizontal hold. That prompts:

The scene flops over
Every few seconds,
And I try to focus in
On the action, plot and dialogue
But I can't.
And I don't.
And I won't
Get up to adjust the set.
All of which is much like today,
When all the action, plot and dialogue
Of my family, friends and colleagues
Ran into each other
And I didn't
And I wouldn't

Get up to help adjust their lives
When I might have
And could have.
But why didn't I?
Why, God, why
Didn't I?

The multi-TV home is the general rule, not the exception. That's one
of the reasons those viewing times are so high. A person doesn't usually
(although you will see there are times when negotiation is needed) have
to negotiate with another person to see a particular show. There is
always a television not in use in the house that the person can turn to—
and on. One of the sets in the house, chances are, is an electronic
antique of sorts. It's an old set that, for whatever reason, no one has
seen fit to leave on the curb on trash day. Fiddling with that antique TV
can evoke a wish like this:

The aerial is bent,
The screen is scratched,
The dial comes off in my hand.
Everything under Your sun, God,
Has its distinctive signs of aging.
May Chronic Complaining
Never be one of mine.
Amen.

Then there is that wonderful adjunct to the television set: the remote-
control unit. This allows us fidgety, short-attention-spanned souls to
jump from station to station and never relinquish our seat. Our
thoughts, at the same time, can jump from the screen to the unseen:

Remote control is a wonderful thing,
The power to flick
From boxing to ballet,
From a swollen, battered face
To a panoply of grace,
Is a wonderfully wondrous thing.
If I only had the flickable power
To switch myself from anger to calm,
From spite to good will that easily,
How much more pleasant my world would be.

Show me, dear God, that, yes, I *do* have that power,
The flickable power that comes from faith in You,
Trusting in Your overwhelming benevolence,
Which, unlike this button in my hand,
Was never,
Is never,
Will never
Be remote.
Amen.

Commercials that have provided me with both a satisfying livelihood and enough cocktail-party fodder to last *this* lifetime, at least (God, don't make me defend advertising throughout eternity!), also offer a splendid opportunity for reflection. That's reflection, not rejection.

They stand in their lots,
Pat their newly buffed hoods
And scream of their deals
Protesting their honesty.

We sit in our chairs,
Pat our newly stuffed selves,
And smirk at their gall,
Smug in *our* honesty.

Almighty Father,
Instill in us both,
Salesman and cynic,
A sense of respect
For each other's intelligence,
Understanding that each
Owes his intelligence
To one loving source,
All-Loving You.
Amen.

Those commercials, many engaging and, yes, some intolerable, are clustered in groups. These commercial breaks vary in length. Depending on the nature of the program, you may see anywhere from two to six commercials in one given—and occasionally, unforgiveable—

stretch. All this has prompted even commercial-loving, advertising-apologetic me to say:

> I have just been asked whether
> My car is roomy enough,
> My wine is dry enough,
> My waist is slim enough.
>
> As I prepare to answer
> Those questions, God,
> Let me quickly toss in
> A thanks to You
> For granting me a life
> Rich enough to include
> A car and wine
> And a waistline
> Worth questioning.

Then there are those commercials for the television shows themselves. They are called promotional announcements—or, for thy hipper understanding, promos. Heavy television viewers see these promos often. Perhaps too often. They promise you entertainment so frequently that you may be tired of the show being touted before it ever has a chance to air. Ah, but those annoying promises can be useful. They may have an even loftier purpose when they lead to a few seconds of self-examination.

> They've been promising me thrills tonight,
> Laughs tomorrow, and a weekend of
> "Wall-to-wall big-league excitement."
> What if You could give me a clue
> As to what to expect out of my life
> Tonight,
> Tomorrow,
> And throughout the weekend?
> Would I strive to work harder
> For Your greater glory
> If I knew just what glory
> Was in store for me?

> If I'm looking for that sort of
> Quid pro quo,
> Thank You, God,
> For *not* letting me know.

These video-inspired chats with God need not necessarily bring out the noblest sides of your being. Not at all. In exploring yourself and a particular dimension of your character, you might touch upon a trait that's not so great. You may cringe. You may be bugged by calling it to mind. You might feel squeamish about wrestling with it. But don't wrestle with it yourself. Talk it over with Him.

> When someone gets attention
> And a mention
> For being, say, the lighting man
> On a shoot-'em-up show,
> Why am I envious
> Of seeing his name on the screen?
> Why do I covet
> His split second of video glory?
> God, help me to understand
> That a credit line with You
> Has a bit more clout
> In the eternal scheme of things
> Than a line crawling
> Up and out of sight
> On a TV screen
> At eleven at night.

> It does,
> Doesn't it?

One of the remarkable aspects of television—and certainly this isn't a profound revelation—is that the medium offers programming that appeals to everyone. The variety of shows seems limitless. Those TV-knockers who say they never watch television because "there's nothing on I'm interested in" are either kidding themselves or are not reading their weekly television schedules. All one needs to do is channel-hop, especially with the number of cable offerings available today, and he's sure to find something to suit his taste. There is also the benefit of finding something that will eventually lead to a conversation with God.

But let's remember, once again, that neither the show itself nor its production value has to be one of immeasurable worth to inspire one to speak to the Creator. No, the show can be as basic as a weekly cooking program.

> In less than thirty minutes
> She has shown me
> How to whip up a lobster newburg
> That will dazzle a table
> Of my most fortunate friends.
> But the dinner would cost *me* a fortune,
> What with the veggies
> And the vinous accompaniment.
> Although I'm understandably impressed
> By the chef's performance
> And the promise that
> I, too, can do it,
> Strike me, God,
> With a spasm of common sense,
> So that I'll remember that
> True friends can read
> Pizza and beer
> As a sign of my
> Hospitality and caring
> Just as easily
> As they can read
> Lobster and Chardonnay.
> Amen.

Then there is the miniseries phenomenon. Since 1976, when the format was introduced, until early in 1986, there had been 106 miniseries presented on America's television networks. Many of these efforts did very well in the ratings, gluing their viewers to the tube night after night. Occasionally one of the dramatic series inspired a viewer to become somewhat introspective. And that resulted in:

> For four consecutive nights
> I have been riveted and rapt,
> Enthralled and engrossed

In the struggles and dreams
Of a fabulous fictional family.

Help me, Father, that I might sustain
As deep and intense an interest
In a real family's struggles;
Namely, mine,
For somewhat longer than
A Sunday through a Wednesday
Between eight and nine.
Amen.

Every so often, a new genre crops up on television. The format wows audiences for a while, sustains healthy ratings, and then fades to become nothing more than an entry in that massive library of television trivia. The blunder/blooper productions are destined to be nostalgic memory. Yes, they have succeeded in entertaining certain numbers of viewers. They have also succeeded certain people take a look at themselves as well as the blunderers.

I roar at their gaffes;
I'm convulsed by their goofs;
How can people make such dumb mistakes?

Hmmm?
Looking at *my* life,
Merciful God,
Have You ever asked Yourself
That same question?

Viewing of local newscasts is on the increase. Viewing of national newscasts is decreasing. Is that significant—and if so, why? As one of those viewers who find themselves more faithful to the local newscasts, it struck me that the answer may not be allegiance to local personalities, but a parochialism that's questionable. Which is a question that's addressed to God:

My eyes grow wider,
My ears perk to attention,
Whenever the local news comes on.
Why does a broken water main downtown
Affect me more than starving Africa?

> Why does a City Council parking ruling
> Intrigue me so much more
> Than a critical UN debate?
> Must I be, God Almighty,
> A citizen of the world
> As well as of this city?
> And if I must,
> How, Good God,
> How?

This television time we share with God (and the networks and the cable stations, too, of course) needn't be spent just for petitions and deftly worded self-deprecations or even for . . . er . . . um . . . sorry . . . stumbling apologies. Thanks are in order too. Always in order and in style. Especially when it's gratitude you're showing to Him.

> The program was made possible,
> The announcer tells me,
> By a grant from
> A huge multinational firm.
>
> May I always remember
> That what *I* am is made possible
> By a grant made gratuitously
> By You.
> Amen.

That thanks, quite clearly, is of a highly personal nature. It's a recognition during a Public Broadcasting show that we are not solely responsible for our good fortune, whatever form that good fortune may happen to take. Gratitude that extends beyond total self-interest may also be inspired by a different sort of television program. Watching a three-hour blockbuster (what earns a movie the right to be called a blockbuster?) film can lead to this kind of thanks:

> We haven't been this close in weeks;
> Our schedules rarely permit us
> A meal together,
> A chat together,
> But now we *are* together

In open-mouthed silence,
Watching Jaboos and Geezinks
Hurtle through space.

Bless my family, Father,
Brought together, temporarily,
By a blockbuster movie.
Hear my prayer
And keep Your loving eyes
On all of us
As we hurtle through life,
And stumble through life,
Skip through,
Trip through,
Lope through
Life.
Amen.

To the station's and the advertisers' delight, you may be watching
that movie for the second or the fourth time. Reruns have become an
accepted, even anticipated, way of viewing life. Can't TV Godtalk become a way of life too? Perhaps it can. Why, maybe a rerun can even
prompt a prayer, one that expresses both human anxiety and aspiration.

I've seen it before.
I know how it ends.
Why am I watching it, then?
Again
And
Again.
Is my time to be spent
Reliving a story
I wasn't that crazy about
In the first place?

Yet I've heard *Your* story
Time and again.
Do I pay as much attention
The eight-hundredth time
As I did the first
Or the fiftieth?

I need reminding, God,
Constant reminding,
That Your story—
And therefore, mine—
Will keep running forever.
Amen.

True, there may be a second or third television set in the house, but
even then there may be occasions when that's still not enough. That's
the case when a family has wide and diverse programming preferences.
Yes, battles over channels happen now and then. And so can a word or
two with God:

I give in.
I give up.
I give over the set
After we've argued at length
Over a Western versus a concert.

But will I learn
From yet another
"I want to watch this—
I want to watch that"
That the problem, God, rests
Not in the shows and their worth,
But in our obsession with "I,"
A point made painfully clear
By the fact that I've used it
Seven . . . whoops . . .
Eight times
In this prayer?

And finally, television may be the finest soporific that man, in his
relentless search for the ultimate tranquillizer, has thus far conceived.
Certainly, for me, television works better than warm milk.

I'm fighting to see it
Through to the finish;
Have I "fingered the perpetrator"?
Have I "nailed down the motive"?

My eyelids are barbell-heavy
And are about to clamp shut
Before the program is over.

Refresh me during this snooze, God,
That I may awake,
Not annoyed to have missed
"The chase"
And
"The collar,"
But grateful that
The plot of *my* life
Is going so well.
Amen.

FRIDAY MORNING

*"Guess Who I Ran into at
the Bank Today, Honey?"*

The confrontations, skirmishes and seemingly irreconcilable standoffs between Almighty God and the almighty dollar have inspired and continue to inspire a wealth (ugh!) of literature. But those writers and readers who maintain that The Maker and money don't belong in the same sentence, let alone under the same roof, might want to spend some time under the roof of the First Hometown Savings and Loan. Under those shingles they might consider the good and Godly activities practiced therein.

Like patience, for example.

Patience while standing in line waiting for the next available teller on the morning after the social security checks have been delivered.

> Were people born seventy years ago
> That much shorter than us
> Latter-day, vitamin-bred wonders?
> Or is it simply age
> That has shortened these women and men
> Who stand in front of me
> With checks fluttering
> In their beautifully bony hands?
> These gentle souls
> Don't fidget and fume

The way that I do.
No, they wait,
Relaxed and content,
With an air of serenity
That comes—or so it seems—
Not from the checks in their hands,
No, God, but, rather,
From You.
Am I right?
Isn't it from you?

Then there is the patience of the veteran employee helping the nervous teller-in-training. The trainee smiles a pained smile at the customer, hoping his vest and mustache make him older and wiser than his years. They don't. His instructor smiles a smile of resignation, her turned-up lips pleading with the customer for forbearance. The customer forbears.

No less exemplary is the patience of the solicitous bank employee who will spend ten minutes punching up the computer to search for a check you carelessly neglected to note in your checkbook.

Patience is a virtuous and divine by-product of just about every visit to the First Hometown Savings and Loan.

As is warm remembrance.

The warm remembrance of a loving grandmother as, fingering through the jewelry in the safe-deposit box, you come upon a cameo brooch she gave you when you turned sixteen.

I've forgotten exactly what her face was like,
It's been so long, so very very long;
Yet I can feel her arms,
Rubbery soft, with a lot of dangling flesh,
Enveloping me in a hug hello,
A hug good-bye,
A hug for no apparent reason at all.
WRONG!
The reason *is* apparent.
Both You and I know why.
What I forgot, however
(And You and the brooch reminded me),
Is just how much

That dear heroic hugger
Really meant to me.

And the warm remembrance of opening a savings account for your little daughter (now a teenage daughter) as you, so directed, make a withdrawal for her so she can go off on a weekend ski trip.

The account was seeded
By birthday money.
Her fifth? Her sixth?
And the midnight generosity
Of the Tooth Fairy,
Who, it seemed, visited her
Every week for three consecutive months.
I remember she objected
To her first bankbook,
Because it was blue
And "blue is for boys."

What a blessing!
Such a blessing!
Isn't that what children are,
According to just about every culture since creation?
Well, I'm beginning to think, God,
As the years do their wizening,
That even a greater blessing than *having* children
Is the memories children leave us with.

Which brings me to ask, Dear God,
That You keep my capacity for remembering keen,
So that, above all other things,
I may remember Who's responsible
For the precious gift of memory
In the first place.
Amen.

But it's not just the expected bank services that suggest God's presence and residence. First Hometown Savings and Loan also provides the space for the community (read humanity) to help and celebrate itself. God, inveterate celebrator that He is, never misses one of these events.

There's the Garden Club Spring Plant Sale, held on the bank's front steps and front lawn. Fuchsia and spider plants hang and sway from the eaves, tantalizing the bank's customers. Rows of reasonably priced blood-red geraniums usually disappear before the bank's 3 P.M. closing time, to reappear on grateful kitchen window sills.

In December, a Boy Scout troop sells Christmas wreaths in the bank's foyer. In the summer, Little League representatives, scuffing their Converses, stand at the bank doors and shyly solicit funds for new uniforms, which a casual glance at the players confirms a need for.

Inside the bank, on a long unobstructed nonbusiness wall, hangs a selection of a local artist's work. The artist is always an amateur one, an art-club member usually, whose landscapes offer perspectives rarely seen in museums and galleries. Are these paintings for sale? Would someone actually hang a Cynthia Sandusky on her living room wall? That's not a rhetorical question. Not when it's addressed to God:

> Would someone actually hang
> A Cynthia Sandusky on her living room wall?
> Someone not related to Cynthia
> By blood or by love?
> There I go again.
> How often do I find myself passing judgment
> On a person's ability
> When I can't paint a stroke
> Or play a note myself?
> Still I'm thankful that *this* time
> (Which I pray is the *last* time)
> I'm putting down someone's efforts
> To You—and only to You,
> Who have, oh so graciously,
> Always kept the knowledge
> Of my shamefully petty thoughts
> To Yourself.

Finally, there is the large wooden container just beyond the table of deposit and withdrawal slips, the table with the theft-proof chained pens, which are always inkless anyway. A community service organization has placed the container there so people may contribute their old eyeglasses for distribution to the nearsighted needy. Good idea. As is the notion of suggesting to God:

May the next pair of eyes
Which look through these glasses
See twice the joys of Your creation
These hazy hazels have.
Amen.

FRIDAY AFTERNOON

Realty vs. Reality

The whole thing began innocently enough, innocence having this knack for beginning monumental things. It was after a late weeknight microwave-salvaged-leftovers dinner: pot roast, frozen potato pancakes and assorted veggies. Both Janice and Phil had been out in the community, each off on his or her pet pro bono project. Then, adequately fed and wispily warmed by a couple of glasses of humble table white, Janice (or was it Phil?) said, "Have you ever thought of us *not* living here?"

"*Not* living here?" responded Phil. (Or was it Janice?) "Not really. We've been here, what, twelve, thirteen years?"

"Fifteen. Fifteen years. Think about it. Phil Junior probably won't be coming home to live here after graduation. Jennifer will be off to college herself soon. With all that, we could really get a better home with three bedrooms instead of four, that being all we really will need, and . . ."

"And this house, I mean, with its location and the way we've kept up the property would be worth . . . what do you think the house would be worth?"

Realtor Number One, called in for an estimate, answered in no time at all, "$280,000."

Realtor Number Two, Janice and Phil feeling that they should get a second opinion, said, "$320,000."

Realtor Number Three, whom Janice and Phil know personally and was a bit peeved when she didn't get asked for an appraisal in the first place, said that both realtors were low. "No problem getting $350,000 for this house," she said.

"$350,000?" gasped Janice and Phil simultaneously, trying not to have their acquaintance, Realtor Number Three, notice that all four of the homeowners' eyes were bouncing around wildly in their sockets.

Janice and Phil asked for verbal corroboration: "You really think you can get $350,000 for this house?"

Realtor Number Three gave it: "No question."

"Okay," said Janice and Phil. "Go to it."

Now, on a windy, rainy Friday afternoon ("Please, God, don't let them see the holes in the drain spout"), Realtor and Potential Buyers stand under a golf umbrella at Janice's (Phil is at work) front door. "Janice," says the Realtor, "let me introduce the Bradleys. Jim is being transferred by his company from Atlanta."

"Come in . . . come in out of the rain . . . I have . . . er . . . I have some phone calls to make. Look around . . . look around . . . and if you have any questions . . . um . . . just give me a . . . uh . . . just give me a yell."

Janice flits out of the foyer (although she would probably be offended if anyone said that she is capable of flitting) and up the stairs, stopping abruptly and turning to wave her arms in an expansive gesture that she hopes is read as "Look around . . . look around." The gesture works. The trio begins to look around.

Upstairs, Janice says to God:

> Why am I stammering
> Like a teenager
> Being examined by a doctor?
> It's my house, not my body,
> That they're looking over.
> Have I grown so attached
> To the brick and wood around me
> That the brick and wood have *become* me?

To which God, without a moment's hesitation, answers, "You figure it out." He does have a habit of saying that, now, doesn't He?

Janice, listening to the footsteps of Realtor Number Three and the Bradleys as they troop through the house, *her* house, follows stealthily, undetectedly behind, one room behind the potential buyers. After twelve, thirteen—no, fifteen—years, Janice knows which floorboards are creaky, and she carefully tiptoes across them. But there is more to her residential memory than which parts of the floor creak. As the trio leaves the kitchen (do all house hunters visit the kitchen first? It seems so) Janice goes into the kitchen, looks around and, taking God's suggestion, tries to "figure it out."

"The kitchen isn't all that big, but it's warm and cheery and . . . well, kitcheny. The baskets probably contribute to the cheeriness. All those baskets hanging on the walls. I wonder if someday some social scientists—they're looking into everything these days—will examine items that hang on walls, windows, doors, that hang from ceilings and roofs, and then make conclusions, draw conclusions about the people who live there. Heh. Maybe they'll invent a whole new science. *Pendology!* The study of the way people live as seen by things they hang. Just look at this kitchen. Sixteen baskets hanging there. All sorts of shapes and sizes and weaves. So what does this tell the pendologist? That we have a preoccupation with abundance? No, I wouldn't say abundance. Plenty. Isn't plenty different from abundance? Isn't sufficient different from surfeit? Of course it is . . . they are. The baskets hang over a table where we eat—graze, in today's vernacular—six to eight times a day. That's plenty, plenty, not abundance, if that's what the pendologists want to read into our hanging baskets."

The people examining the house leave the dining room clucking what sound to be positive clucks. Janice follows secretly, taking her free-flowing "you figure it out" exercise with her into the just vacated room.

"The kitchen, with all those hanging baskets, is the main eating room. Not dining room . . . eating room. This is the dining room, with the tapestry and the medieval sconces (imitation, hardly fifteenth-century). Okay, so what significance, what pendological meaning, do these dining room trappings have? What? That Phil and I are dreamers? That we have had wild fantasies over legendary meals in this room? That somehow the two of us fancy ourselves as mistress and master of our split-level castle and that outside that big picture window we don't see squirrels running around, but unicorns? Incorrigible dreamers, huh? Is that what the hanging tapestry means?"

But, moving into the living room, Janice concludes, "But that fantasy theory doesn't mesh with what the living room looks like . . . with what hangs here. Sure there are the Manet and Monet reproductions. Phil and I are both wild about the Impressionists, but what dominates the walls? Larssons. Carl Larssons. The Swede who was a kind of Scandinavian Norman Rockwell. Larsson, who painted these very homey scenes . . . domestic life . . . his own country home. Okay, social scientists specializing in hanging things, what do you draw from this . . . from the Carl Larssons? That Phil and I are caught up in this paradox? The medieval fantasy of the dining room? The homey reality of the living room? A pendological paradox?

"In *this* room," Janice mindspeaks to herself and her imaginary scientists, "you're really going to be thrown off. Nothing hanging here, in our bedroom, but the chandelier. Sure, it's no ordinary chandelier, but that's the only hanging object here. A lovely thing, isn't it? All those prisms reflecting the lights of those tiny bulbs. But those tiny bulbs have to be replaced so often. And the chandelier is a real dust collector. Okay, does the chandelier and the flickering lights bring us more into the fantasy—the Cinderella's-ball sort of camp, rather than the domestic-reality camp?

"Will this room be consistent with that theory?" she asks, heading into Jennifer's room a few seconds after Realtor and Bradleys have left it. "Romantic, isn't it? Is that what you read into Jennifer's soft-sculpture collection? Wonderful, aren't they? Dreamy? See the ice-cream cone hanging from the ceiling? Soft and satiny. Over there, from the canopy of the bed, a plush rainbow. The mere fact the bed has a canopy brings you into fantasyland, doesn't it? Cinderella or, better yet, Sleeping Beauty. That's right: Sleeping Beauty sleeping under all those fat little fabric stars. How's that for romantic? We *are* a bunch of dreamers, aren't we?

"And this, ace dreamer, chief dreamer of them all," Janice concludes as she steps over a pair of sneakers and into B.J.'s room. Larry Bird and Dwight Gooden on the wall. B.J. can't make up his mind which of the two he wants to be. Or one of those wrestlers with the crazy names. Junkyard Dog and Hillbilly Something-or-Other. Now, isn't that pendological proof . . . as conclusive as you guys can get . . . that we are all dreamers in this family? And if we *are*, if I am really a romantic, at heart a domestic/romantic/fantasizing . . ."

Janice's internalized monologue, her pendological soul-searching, is interrupted by Mrs. Bradley. She and her husband and Realtor Number Three have concluded their inspection. Mrs. Bradley clasps her hands (is she a concert singer?) and says, "You have a lovely home, a *truly* lovely home. We are interested, *truly* interested. Tell me, is the price negotiable?"

"Negotiable?" thinks Janice. "Is the price negotiable? Are the baskets and the tapestry, the Larssons and the Gooden, the ice-cream cone and the chandelier, dust and all, flickering lights and all, negotiable?"

"No, they're not," she replies brusquely and a bit too emphatically, for Mrs. Bradley visibly stiffens her shoulders and says, *"They're* not?"

"I mean *it,* the price, is not negotiable."

"Oh, that's a shame, *truly* a shame. Your home *is* lovely, but I'm afraid, *we're* afraid, $350,000 is more than we care to spend on a home."

And Realtor, flashing Janice a penetrating "how could you?" farewell glare, and the Bradleys, shaking their heads, leave. Janice shuts the door. She takes a deep breath, and as she does, Janice hears God say to her, "See, you figured it out."

FRIDAY NIGHT

An Early Movie and a Late, Late Night

If you are a city dweller, there might have been paragraphs and even pages you've come across thus far that have prompted you to say, "So what's so especially exclusively suburban about that? We do things like that in the city, too."

I cannot deny that there may have been some in-town and out-of-town societal commonalities presented here, and we're about to see another universal activity. Yet the way the suburbanite and the urbanite behave during these universal activities—especially this one—most assuredly differentiates one from the other.

Friday night quite often is unwind-at-a-movie night both in the burbs and in the city. Frequently husband and wife, friend and friend, who haven't seen much of each other in the hurly-burly of the business week, meet for an early movie right after work on Friday night. This happens both just down the street from one's midtown office—and right after the commuter debarks from the train and steps into his verdant suburban oasis once more.

Off to a relaxing movie.

Off to an entertaining flick.

Off to a long waiting line.

Here is where you'll find the difference between the urban and the suburban. The movie line. The film playing in both locales may be the same, but the attitude and mentality of the people in the movie lines will be vastly different.

For one thing, *suburban moviegoers are friendlier.* People waiting in line in the city will do antisocial things like bury their heads in a newspaper or even a book as they wait for the ticket window to open. They will rarely speak to one another, even to their own mates-in-waiting. On the other hand, in the suburbs, the chatter in the movie line is ceaseless. Hardly anyone waits in silence. Yet the conversation in suburban lines tends to be about the new drapes and the new crepe restaurant, about the kids' camp and damp basements, about the proposed dump or the jump in realty tax. My point is not that the conversation is about a whole slew of subjects; it's that no one in a suburban movie line talks about the film he or she is about to see. That's because of this second difference between suburban moviegoer and city moviegoer: *the suburban moviegoer is cinematically insecure.* In the suburbs, as the patrons of the previous showing are filing out, listen to what the people waiting in line are saying.

"Was it any good?"

"Did you like it?"

"How was it?"

Suburban moviegoers crave to know they have made the right choice. (That's true about more than movies, isn't it, God?) In this particular case, to corroborate their judgment suburban moviegoers will accost outgoing patrons with the brashness and aggressiveness of a TV reporter at a disaster site. The city moviegoer, on the other hand, couldn't care less. He has made a decision and he'll stick to it, come hell or high boredom. I've often wondered what a suburban moviegoer's reaction would be if an exiting patron yelled out, "Wow! What a stinker! Was that ever a turkey!" Would the person waiting in line stay in line, or would he slink quietly away?

Suburban moviegoers save places in line more willingly than do city moviegoers. It's not because suburban moviegoers are, by and large, friendlier, although our first finding tends to conclude that. No. It's because the driver of the car in suburbia has to circle the parking lot, the neighborhood, and sometimes the entire village to find a place to park. His space in the movie waiting line must be saved—and it's usually saved by a self-sacrificing, and quite often shivering, Someone Else. We can't honestly say that searching for an empty space in a crowded parking lot is among life's ten most frustrating frustrations. Not really.

Yet the weaving in and out, the snaking and the braking, the vrooming and the fuming, do give one a chance to say:

> Writers, both heavy and hack,
> Tell us You've a role for everyone in life.
> I appreciate being included in Your plot,
> But must *my* role be
> To endlessly
> Drive around a parking lot?

In this regard the city dweller has a distinct advantage over the suburbanite. The city dweller can get to the movie house simply by going down the elevator and around the block. And since he believes everybody should be able to do the same thing (which in the city everybody just about can) the city moviegoer will resist saving a place for anybody—stranger, kith or kin.

And finally, *suburban moviegoers are less patient.* It is accurate to report that suburban moviegoers will not wait in line as long as city moviegoers will. No doubt about it. The suburban moviegoer's Queue Quotient is woefully low. If the line is long or the wait is over fifteen minutes, the typical suburban cinemaphile will immediately opt for a margarita and a chili relleno, rather than a David Lean epic. The city moviegoer, however, will stand in line to see that epic for almost as long as it takes for the film to run.

Another thought about going to the movies; this thought is a little bit convoluted, but bear with me: This monotheist is compelled to confess that he rather misses the opportunity to refer to a particular drink or a specific dish as being the drink or the food of the gods. I was an impressionable eight or nine when I first learned that nectar was the drink of the gods. The only nectar I had known prior to that shard of lore was the apricot nectar with which my mother occasionally surprised me at breakfast. As I said, I was an impressionable eight or nine. Also an imaginative eight or nine. I conjured up this image of all those flowing-togaed deities on Mt. Olympus passing around a jumbo can of apricot nectar, copiously pouring the heavy sticky liquid into their enormous goblets. With all the drinks in the world at their sacred disposal, apricot nectar seemed a peculiar choice, but, then again, gods are different from us mere mortals, I concluded at eight or nine.

Now, some decades later, this monotheist rather wishes that God, our one Creator, our sole deity, would need—or, at least, condescend to crave occasionally—some sort of earthly gustatorial delight. Betcha He wouldn't choose apricot nectar. Betcha my last *escudo* that, should it ever happen, the food that God would choose would be . . . popcorn.

Popcorn?

Popcorn.

Why popcorn?

Easy. Can you think of any other food with as many spiritual qualities and contemplative cues associated with it?

Contemplative cues?

What's a contemplative cue?

Well, consider the corn plant itself. There is something about the way corn stretches to the sky that connotes ambition, a tugging, pulling, yearning for growth, and with that growth, fulfillment. The analogy is fairly obvious. It is perhaps a little too, too wincingly, painfully obvious.

Nevertheless, the cornstalk does have a nobility to it, a dignity that it manages to maintain throughout its productive life and, unlike almost all other plants, even after it has been dug up or hacked down. Even the spent cornstalk remains firm and proud as it adorns pastures and, yes, even suburban front lawns late into the autumn.

All this while munching your way through a bucket of popcorn?

Why not? It's a big bucket.

And how about this? Is there a more prolific veggie on God's created earth than corn? Think of the kernels on each ear, the ears on each stalk, the stalks in each row, the rows in each acre. Poets of the distant and the not-so-distant past might have been better off had they contemplated (and rhymed and romanticized) about kernels of corn, rather than grains of sand. Metaphors and similes and meandering streams of consciousness come much easier with corn—if one sets one's mind to it. After all, corn is a living thing; sand isn't. Corn can do so many things. The best sand can do is shift.

Then too, I think God would especially like popcorn—and consider it His food—because of popcorn's exuberance, the loud way it erupts and shows itself off. Like the creator of just about anything—a song, a sand castle, a snowman—I have to assume that God, too, wants to see His creations celebrated. And popcorn certainly *is* celebrated. In fact, it's *doubly* celebrated. Popcorn celebrates itself, bouncing off the popper's walls, the muffled bursts translated into "I'm here. I'm complete. I'm ready."

And then we popcorn lovers begin celebrating.

Consider how we do that.

The celebration is usually—not always, but usually—in a dimly lit theater. Before the movie even begins, we are gleefully digging into our buttery bucket—or, worse, our "buttery-flavor" bucket. "Buttery-flavor" is the greasy euphemism that's used for that greasy substitute for butter that's all too prevalent in movie theaters today. At any rate, real butter or "buttery-flavor," as we dig in we muse either on the movie about to be screened or something about to happen in our life—if not the moment we leave the movie house, then tomorrow or soon thereafter. Popcorn and anticipation go together.

So do popcorn and human reaction. What other food is associated with a visible, audible, palpable emotion every single time you partake of it? Beer is *sometimes* accompanied by tears or laughter; popcorn is almost *always* accompanied by tears or laughter, gasps of fright or squeals of delight, moans or howls, gulps of disgust, sighs of sadness— and a variety of cheers for a whole array of different last-second rescues and/or plot resolutions.

Popcorn enjoys a metaphysical bond with humanness.

Popcorn is also the world's most social food.

Consider that popcorn is the only food shared while eaten more often than it is eaten alone. Since that is so, the act of sharing brings people together, even if that togetherness is no more poignant than two greasy fingers touching and sliding off each other way down in the bottom of the bucket. True, it's not a very deep intimacy, but an intimacy nonetheless. Friends, we have to grab our moments of sharing wherever and however we can.

Fine. Now that we have shared our popcorn, now that we have shared Woody Allen and Mia Farrow, the houselights go on and we see . . . what do we see? . . . whom do we see? Why, our neighbors from up the hill. And our friends from The Club. And our travel agent and her husband.

"This must be the in thing to do."

"I just love Woody."

"So do I, but I'm always a little let down."

"That's funny. So am I. I always expect more of him."

"You guys had dinner yet?"

"No, Jeb just got in from the airport and . . ."

"Anyone for pizza?"

"Who's not for pizza?"

"I sorta like the burgers at . . ."

"Yeah. Pizza. Want to meet at Torchia's?"

"How about La Manda's?"

"Why don't you all come over to our place. We'll relax . . . we'll call for pizza . . . have a drink . . ."

"Why make all that work for yourself?"

"What work?"

"Good idea," says Jeb, who just got in from New Orleans with a plane change in Atlanta.

I'm all for the idea too. But before we can carry out Operation Pizza, this:

> I understand that in *Your* cast, God,
> Everyone is a star,
> But could You tell this dumb actor
> Where I parked my car?

When letter writing was in vogue and William James seemed to be riveted to his old escritoire day and night, he wrote: "Human beings are born into this little span of life of which the best thing is its friendships and intimacies, and soon their places will know them no more, and yet they leave their friendships and intimacies with no cultivation, to grow as they will by the roadside, expecting them to 'keep' by force of mere inertia."

James was certainly no burbologist. Had he been, he would have had second thoughts—or better, yet, no thoughts at all—before putting that thought to paper. Lack of friendship cultivation? Not in the suburbs. Not at all.

James, too, might have been invited to "come over to our place . . . we'll relax . . . call for pizza . . . have a drink" and witnessed friendships and intimacies being cultivated laughingly, loudly, unpretentiously. By his third slice of a pepper-and-pepperoni pizza (extra oregano) and a second glass of Hearty Burgundy, James would have concluded that these impromptu get-togethers are magnificent exercises in bonding. He probably would have joined right in with the nonagendized psychodrama. He probably would have participated, mozzarella caught in his teeth, in an evening in which God's creations affirmed their own humanity by appreciating the humanity of others.

Reflect on the octet that decide to share a bite and a few hours.

Al and Clarisse. Al has been unwilling, for nearly a year now, to accept the fact that a merger of his firm with another, larger company, has made Al "redundant." Being unwilling to accept that fact, Al is not only unemployed but not even looking for work all that actively. Clarisse is heroically unselfish. She has, ungrudgingly, taken a job as a receptionist in a health clinic.

Ursula and Jeb. Ursula, with a very strong, big kick serve for a woman, has won the ladies singles tennis title at The Club for the past three years. Jeb is just in from New Orleans with a plane change in Atlanta. Jeb is on the road a lot.

Suzyn and Harold. Suzyn with a z? And a y? The spelling may appear to be a little pretentious, but there's nothing else pretentious about Suzyn. In fact, she's rather self-effacing and charming and always appears to be interested in what other people say and think. That quality, among others, has helped Suzyn's travel agency to become one of the most successful in the county. Harold is a philosophy professor, a Kierkegaard scholar. That is, he is a philosophy professor by day. By night—or whenever he is within earshot of an alarm—Harold is an avid and devoted volunteer fireman.

And there's, yes, She and I.

Hour One of our impromptu get-together is taken up by communal eating ("Anyone ready for another slice? . . . mushroom? . . . how about mushroom? . . . somebody must have ordered mushroom, but nobody's eating it . . ."), communal reviewing of the movie everyone has just seen ("Not one of his best . . . but Mia continues to surprise me . . . she's one terrific actress, isn't she?"), Suzyn talking about Iceland as a relatively inexpensive offbeat tourist spot, Ursula talking about ice-skating on the frozen rivers of her native Sweden, and Me, a.k.a. I, trying to get the #&@!! ice maker to work.

Hour Two sees and hears Clarisse talking about all the people coming into the clinic concerned about AIDS, Harold talking about one of the teaching fellows in his department who has been diagnosed as having AIDS, and Ursula wondering out loud what any of the eight would do if a son told them he is a homosexual.

Hour Three, which begins just after midnight, has Jeb yawning and saying, "Yaaahhhh . . . it's been a brutal week, just brutal. We'd better get going."

This draws a reaction from Al. "Oh, I remember brutal weeks. What I wouldn't do for a brutal week or two again. No, I'll probably never see one, never see a brutal week again." The sarcastic stress on the word "brutal" isn't meant to be a put-down of Jeb. It's not *meant* to be, but it might be read as such. But it's not. It's just the beery babbling of a disconsolate out-of-work soul.

But Hour Three is also Harold saying, "Al, did you ever give any thought to teaching?"

"Teaching?"

"That's right. On a college level."

"What could I teach?"

"Advertising . . . marketing. At my place, for example, we have people teaching in those disciplines whose only knowledge of the subjects has been gleaned from books. Look at what you can bring to the party. What is it? Twenty, twenty-five years of first-hand experience? And all your success stories and all those case histories you've told us about through the years."

Hour Three is She taking Harold's suggestion and running with it too. More than running with it—steamrollering it. "That's a wonderful idea. Isn't that a wonderful idea, folks? Okay, everyone . . . think of who you all know at the various colleges in the area. I mean, besides Harold, who'll handle any and all possibilities at *his* school, right, Harold? Now let's think of any deans, trustees, those kinds of people. Tonight we launch Al's new career . . . Academic Al's new career."

And how does Hour Three conclude? With a fire alarm. And Harold dashing out in response to it.

Hour Four begins with Jeb once again saying that they must be going. This time, however, everyone, in as close to unison as four hours of partying can prompt, says, "No." They all agree they must wait until Harold comes back from his call and reports in. Why's that? Natural curiosity? Solicitude? It doesn't matter which. It doesn't matter what's the excuse to keep them there. The people now want to be together. They want to stay and talk.

They talk about what they're doing: waiting. How they have waited for spouses. Funny waits. Frightening waits. Harrying waits at fogged-in airports and commuter train stations. And then the conversation turns to waiting for children, especially waiting for children to come home at night.

She says: "I've told my kids, no matter what time it is when they come in, no matter how late, be sure to come into my room and kiss me good night."

Clarisse: "How do you tell one of your children's kisses from your husband's?"

I: "I don't kiss after midnight."

Which stirs sleepy Jeb to say, "You must be a barrel of laughs on New Year's Eve."

Which sets everybody off to reminiscing about memorable New Year's Eves they have experienced. Now no one, not even Jeb, just back from New Orleans with a plane change in Atlanta, feels like leaving. No one wants to dam up those waves of memory that are rolling in one after the other. They are sharing glorious yesterdays. They are sharing, yes, intimacies.

Those long, long nights that extend into the wee-est of hours need not disintegrate into the spite and spleen of *Who's Afraid of Virginia Woolf?*. Just the opposite. Long suburban nights can be a coming together, rather than a wrenching apart. Like this long suburban night.

The subjects of conversation, streaming almost subconsciously, can be a mix of the serious and the silly. Sometimes serious can flow into silly and vice versa without the conversationalists even realizing it. In fact, when the hour gets ridiculously late and the wine or the beer or the just plain shoes-off comfort has taken effect, silliness can be joyfully sweet.

As it is at Hour Five. It is now a little after 2 A.M. and Harold returns, smelling of smoke. Before he can be barraged by questions, Harold himself offers up the bulletin in staccato, reportorial fashion: "Apartment on Pine. Smoking in bed. Set fire to his Sealy. Light property damage. Man treated at hospital and released."

Al, no longer preoccupied with the fact that he's redundant, reflects, "Since I was a little kid I've been crazy about the smell of smoke. So was my father. We loved the smell of smoked anything—bacon, turkey, salmon, the fireplace."

Suzyn asks, "Even smoky philosophy profs?"

"That's a first for me . . . I never got a whiff of smoky philosophy prof before."

Clarisse adds, "Don't be offended, Harold, but I have to say, I prefer . . . gardenia."

"Gardenia?" say I, pouring myself a bit more wine, the thought striking me that I don't need a designated driver tonight. I'm in my own designated house.

The thought that struck me now runs away with me. "That's inter-

esting, you mentioning gardenia, Clarishe, ah, Clarisse. I wonder . . .
I wonder . . . if we . . . if all of us . . . were to be a flower, yeah, a
flower, what would each of us choose to be. Clarisse . . . is that what
you'd be . . . a gardenia?"

Clarisse: "Gardenias are fine. I love the smell. I mean, I love the
smell . . . for a while. But I don't know as I would like to go around
smelling like a gardenia all the time. There's this other thing about
gardenias that wouldn't thrill me either. When they're cut, they turn
brown very quickly."

Al: "But you love to have a tan."

Clarisse: "Tan, yes, but I don't want to be gardenia brown. No, I
think I would rather be a gladiola. Or is it gladiolus? Whatever, I'd like
to be tall, certainly taller than I am now, and a glad is so . . . so
ramrod straight. I'd love it."

Jeb: "Hyacinth! Hyacinth for me! Ever go into a room with a whole
mess of hyacinths in it? You take a deep whiff and it's like beer. Really
. . . I'm not kidding you. Smell for yourself. Hyacinths smell like
beer."

Clarisse: "And that's what you would like to do . . . spend your
whole life smelling like beer?"

Jeb: "Ah, well . . . um . . . maybe not . . . ah . . ."

Ursula: "I think I would like to be a crocus. I want to be the first
flower to appear after the snow, after the winter."

I: "That must be the Swedish in you."

Ursula: "Perhaps, but there is always a feeling of wonderful surprise
whenever you see your first crocus. I would like people to have the same
feeling when they see me."

Al: "I don't know if this qualifies, but I'd like to be an apple blossom."

She: "Sure it qualifies. It's a flower. But why an apple blossom, Al?"

Al: "It's kind of for the same reason Ursula wants to be a crocus.
When you're an apple blossom you're part of . . . of an event. I mean,
the whole tree erupts in us apple blossoms. There are thousands of us.
When we open up people ooh and ahh. We apple blossoms attract wows
and gasps and oohs and ahhs."

I: "And bees."

Al: "Yeah, bees, too, but that's part of the process. The great thing is
that all of us apple blossoms are part of this spectacular bigger thing. I
bet each of us apple blossoms would consider himself tickled pink just

being there, on the tree. It'd be like the Super Bowl of nature. We'd all be . . . each little one of us . . . completing a spectacle, part of a spectacle. I'm probably all over the lot and not making much sense, but, that's it, that's what I'd want to be: an apple blossom.

She: "I'd want to be an iris, a very deep blue iris. Are there any of you who are into flower language? Anybody study what flowers symbolize? I read somewhere that the iris stands for hope, but that's not the reason I'm picking it. I love the blue of irises. Van Gogh and I love them. You just don't find those particular blues anywhere else in nature. At least, I haven't."

Suzyn: "Do you know what the camellia symbolizes? I see myself as a camellia."

She: "No, I don't. It's a very pretty flower."

Harold: "I went to high school with a girl named Camellia."

Suzyn: "You did?"

Harold: "Okay, okay, it probably sounds ridiculous, but the name stuck with me even though I probably can't remember the five or six Caroles I went to school with."

Suzyn: "What flower would *you* choose to be, Harold?"

Harold pauses. He thinks. He thinks a long time.

Al: "C'mon, Harold, we haven't got all night."

Jeb, who has long forgotten that he flew in from New Orleans with a plane change in Atlanta: "Oh, yes we have."

Harold: "I don't know really, but it would be a climbing plant."

Clarisse: "That's the fireman in you."

Ursula: "Or the philosopher . . . with lufty aspirations." (Although Ursula has been in the country for some time every so often a verbal Scandinavian vestige will crop up, like "lufty" for "lofty.")

Harold: "Fireman, philosopher, whatever you want to ascribe it to, I'd like to be a climbing plant. And now that I think of it, I'd like to be a clematis."

Al: "Isn't that clam juice mixed with tomato juice?"

Harold: "Not bad, Al. But no, clematis is a flower that grows on a twiggy sort of vine that crawls up whatever it's planted near . . . a lamppost, a mailbox, the side of a house. The flowers come in different colors, but I think I would choose to be a *red* clematis."

Suzyn: "Fire-engine red?"

Harold: "Fire-engine red."

Al turns to me and says, "And now that you've started all this, and now that you've heard all of us, just what would *you* like to be?"

I: "I really don't know specifically what flower I would want to be. I'm not sure, but I *am* sure of this . . ."

Al: "Yes?"

I: "I want to be a perennial."

And Harold, who has chosen to be a clematis, a perennial, says, "Don't we all . . . don't we all."

Now, who dares to think that God hasn't been with the eight of us tonight?

SUBURBAN RITES

To be sure, legions of suburbanites like to celebrate their neighbor God in a formal fashion for some period of weekend time. There are many venues for this celebration/adoration. There are temples, homes, churches, and converted buildings, the most notable trend in that regard being the renovation of movie theaters into houses of worship. Of course, the length of formal group worship varies depending on the nature of the service and the predilections of both the officiator and the worshipers.

But we are not going to cover formal worship here. We will move through the weekend with Phil and Janice and others without specifically describing or commenting on how they may communicate with God in a public forum if they have chosen to do so. Our premise, as we hope we've made clear by this late date in the week, is that God, as a constant and close-by fellow townie, can be communicated with—and even privately worshiped—in dozens upon dozens of suburban moments and situations other than the programmed weekend worship events.

Wait. We are not suggesting that private worship is better than public. We are not saying that a chat with God while you're raking leaves is more meaningful and uplifting than, say, an ecumenical candlelight service on the village green. We *are* saying, however, that to overlook the Creator in the course of normal suburban life is comparable to passing by the school crossing guard without a greeting, or going through the checkout counter without a few pleasantries with the cashier. God is just as much a suburban fixture as are the crossing guard and the checkout clerk. God is as willing to listen to a fellow villager as is Sid, the long-suffering bartender at the Town Square Pub. God is as ready to lend a hand as the twenty-four-hour-on-call folks of the village ambulance corps. And if we're willing to listen carefully, God is as eager to talk to us about our wants and needs as is Jean, the loan officer of First Hometown Savings & Loan.

SATURDAY MORNING

Taking God to Task . . .
After Task . . . After Task

There can be little argument that Saturday morning is the most fre-
netic chunk of the suburban week. White-collar nine-to-fivers are generally home on Saturday morning. So are schoolchildren. Errands,
chores, tasks (pick your favorite word; none of them are glamorous)
have been, because of all kinds of other family duties and obligations,
put off until this particular weekend morning.

Now is the time to "make the rounds." Yet Phil wonders, and God
hears him wondering:

> Does anyone say
> "make the rounds" any more?
> (The phrase is one of the
> Memory treasures my father left me.)
> Well, here I am about to
> "make the rounds" again,
> My Saturday morning routine,
> Chore after chore,
> Whose successful completion
> Brings me home again,
> Having come full circle,
> Completing the circle,
> The perfect *O.*

Will You do or say something
When I'm about to complete the round
Of this great gift, Life?
Oh, not so I'd have a chance
To change something
Or rearrange something, but . . .

. . . who am I kidding?
Of course so I'd have a chance
To change something
Or rearrange something.

Having gathered and sorted and counted six shirts, two suits (press only) and Janice's blouse and dress (special attention to underarms), Phil tiptoes through the house and down the stairs in order not to waken anyone this early on a Saturday morning. But somebody is already awake. The TV in the den is on. Before the sun has had time to reach treetop height, B.J. lies sprawled in front of the tube.

"What are you doing up? You could have slept much later today."

"I could have, but I didn't. If I slept any longer I would have missed the wrestling."

"Wrestling? You have to be kidding. Wrestling is all a put-on."

And Phil's spitting image spits, "I know, Dad, but what a neat put-on!"

Wrestling: The Neat Put-On. Phil doubts that the wrestling powers that be would go along with that descriptive, but the rebirth of the "sport" has been phenomenal, and Phil thinks about it as he drives to the cleaner's. It's quite a drive, to the next town in fact, Phil having forsaken the four in-town cleaners because none of them could meet his stringent requirements for ironing shirt collars.

Actually Phil does sneak a few minutes every so often in front of televised wrestling. He has plenty of opportunity. There seems to be a show on every day on some station or other, especially on the cable channels. A galaxy of grunters has become as first-name, nickname familiar and acceptable to Americans as have Bill Cosby and Diane Sawyer. The wrestling champs, like Hulk Hogan and Tito Santana, are bland behemoths compared to some of the wild characters who drop into homes on a daily basis with, of course, reverberating thuds.

There's George "The Animal" Steele, the bald baddie with the green tongue who's known for eating the stuffing out of the turnbuckle pads on the ring. One of Phil's favorites (yes, he's watched enough to even have favorites) had been Hillbilly Jim, who had trained under (perhaps an inappropriate expression) Hulk Hogan. Hillbilly Jim had had a promising career until that giant from San Francisco, Brutus Beefcake, broke his leg. Ah, but Hillbilly hasn't given up the game altogether. He now manages overpowering, overwhelming, and overalled Uncle Elmer.

But what would happen if Phil—and people like him—had a wrestling hero they could really and truly identify with? Junkyard Dog, The Iron Sheik and The Missing Link are cartoon characters in the flesh. And a lot of flesh. Since televised wrestling is now so available in suburban homes, what if Phil and all of us had a wrestler for people with a Macho Ratio somewhat lower than a Fiji Island warrior or a five-hundred-pound farm boy or an ex-Marine drill instructor has?

What if we inveterate (and God-crafted that way) fantasizers had . . . Suburban Man to root for?

Suburban Man! He would be an instant idol (no, God, not in *that* sense) for all of us in the blessed burbs. Imagine Suburban Man entering the ring wearing a three-piece suit and specially designed wing-tip wrestling shoes. He would doff his jacket and tie, but keep his vest on during the entire match. Meanies would, of course, try to pop the buttons off Suburban Man's vest, but goodness and his powerful forearm smash would prevail.

Entry into the ring is important to establish the persona of every wrestler. Suburban Man would step into the ring waving his attaché case wildly, eager to do battle with the most fiendish of opponents. No one would be safe from Suburban Man's rage. After all, he has spent the entire day at the office. He needs an outlet for his seven and a half hours of pent-up, corporation-provoked fury.

Suburban Man, as all wrestlers worth their salty sweat must, would have to have his own patented hold or move. It might be the Trash Slam, the move that has Suburban Man lifting his opponent high over his head and slamming him mercilessly to the mat. That is the same move as Suburban Man lifting the trash bag and slamming it into his garbage container on collection day.

Or Suburban Man may be known for what his coach labels the Commuter Shoulder Block. This is a fierce weapon, a violent block that sends Suburban Man's opponents flying across the ring. Suburban man would have perfected this maneuver on the train platform, where he feels compelled to shoulder fellow commuters away from the door when the train pulls into the station.

There is the possibility that Suburban Man could develop a move that no other wrestler could ever copy or preempt. This might be the Bouncie-Bouncie-on-My-Shoulders. The inspiration for this devastating move is the village parade. Suburban Man takes his child to the parade, putting the little nipper up on his shoulders and bouncing him gently up and down. But when Suburban Man lists his opponent up on his shoulders and bounces his opponent up and down, there's nothing gentle about it at all. Suburban Man's rivals would live in dread of this move, fearing the moment when they might be hoisted and bounced and bounced and bounced and then dashed to the canvas and pinned for yet another Suburban Man victory.

Wow! Would we love that sort of action, that kind of hero. If the czars of wrestling only knew how even more successful they might be if they were to give the people in the suburbs their own rooting interest: Suburban Man.

But on this Saturday morning the suburban man (small s, small m) has tasks to perform that don't require the strength and stamina of Suburban Man (capital S, capital M). The first such task is dropping off the clothes at the dry cleaner's. That's Norm.

Norm is one of those people whom other people, like Phil, find hard to take at face value. "Can he really *like* what he's doing? When Norm goes on talking about different fruit and grease stains, does he actually find them interesting? And working in that unbearably hot shop must be murder. How can he stand it? Is he a bit dense? How in the world anybody would like to do or be what Norm does and is is beyond me!"

Remember Hirer Haughtiness, that unpleasant idiom in which Janice addressed some service people back on Monday afternoon? Well, Phil's attitude toward Norm the dry cleaner is related to Hirer Haughtiness. It may even be more insidious. It's Uppity Pity, the real or imagined sympathy for one of a lower, and supposedly meaner, station in life.

How often have we tsk-tsk-ed our concern for someone whose job or whose lot we felt bad about. Or *thought* we should feel bad about? Or thought we should express our views to someone about feeling bad about?

Some examples of Uppity Pity:

"Driving a cab at night in the city! Oh, boy, is that ever the worst job in the world!"

"My cleaning lady sometimes brings her daughter along with her to help out. Imagine a twelve-year-old, down on her knees, scrubbing bathroom floors. What in the world does she have to look forward to in life?"

"I just don't understand how Norm can take it. In the summer the temperature in there must get to 120 degrees easily."

Yes, there may be some genuine concern tucked into those syllables of expressed pity, but since the lines are spoken by the likes of Phil (and so many others of us) to our fellow human beings, isn't the import of those words really, "Ain't it great? Aren't we sitting pretty? We sure got the long straw in the draw of life, didn't we?"

Oh, we will deny ever having those kinds of uppity thoughts, but they are natural to have. It's part of our genetic frailty (built in at the point of manufacture) to feel that way sometimes. Comparisons can't be avoided. But comparisons can help us to grow, rather than prompt us to crow.

How?

Here's a rather offbeat how.

I've often felt that one of the great unexploited clichés of our language is "There but for the grace of God go I." Think of all the times we have passed a blind beggar, a legless war veteran or a bag lady and instinctively mindmuttered that phrase. Wouldn't it be worth a 24-point headline—not to mention being something of a sociological hoot—if we who lapse into Uppity Pity on occasion could have the power to give up some of our God-given graces to those we've just labeled and lamented as being less fortunate?

It would work this way: We're walking down the street and a scruffy guy in soiled clothing stops us. He asks, slurringly, "Can you shpare some shange for coffee anna roll?"

His speech and breath suggest coffee isn't exactly what he has in mind. Now, rather than snapping your customary "Nah, nah, no change" and striding off muttering, "There but for the grace of God go I," you actually say to God, "Okay, You've been so generous to me with Your graces, let me cash one in for this guy. Let's give one of my graces to the guy so he'll get off the hooch."

And just as easy as that, you could transfer a grace from yourself to the man you just pitied. The man would go on the wagon and you, who had been graced with, for example, a beautiful singing voice, would no longer be able to carry a tune. Of course, this world-class act of selflessness would need the cooperation of creation's only Grace Giver, but He just might be interested in this sort of sublime trade-in. A thought. Just a thought.

With just a little bit of effort on our part, Saturday morning can crackle with thoughts, some as fuzzily mystical as that grace-trade-in idea, and others as mistily rueful as "God, I wish our kids were still young."

Phil, eating his sausage McMuffin (with egg) at the McDonald's next to Norm's dry-cleaning establishment, watches a couple of tables of tykes and their accompanying adults and says, "God, I wish our kids were still young."

God asks, "Why?"

Phil has to think why. It takes him most of his McMuffin before he can come up with anything that resembles a logical answer:

> We cherish, they say, the innocence of children,
> And when that innocence fades,
> As it inevitably does,
> We mourn the loss of that simpler time.
> Yet I think I miss
> The *silliness* of young children
> Even more than their vaunted innocence,
> Their freedom to make faces
> And strange noises and sounds,
> The license they take
> To jump on chairs,
> Roll wildly on floors,
> Sensing that we find
> Their unashamed silliness
> One of Your more endearing
> Gifts to us.

From Norm's and McDonald's, onto the Lethe Brushless Car Wash. Here Phil and car owners like him find two minutes and twenty-eight seconds of stress-scrubbing. Some time back, Phil became aware that tensions brought on by any number of things could be alleviated by driving a car through the car wash. When anxiety brought on by any number of stresses would attack Phil, he'd drive up and hear those soothing words "Neutral . . . no brakes." Those three words, shouted by the car-wash attendant through Phil's rolled-up window, would immediately have a sedative effect. Phil and his car would then be hitched onto the conveyor chain that would pull them through the tunnel of tranquillity.

Not that Saturday morning is an especially stressful time of week, unless one considers a late-morning visit to the dentist somewhat stressful. No, the stresses of the week have been built up to the point where, by Saturday morning, general angst (wasn't he a prominent figure during the Battle of the Bulge?) has overcome Phil. But there is relief, blessed welcome relief. The rinse water gushing over the car, its soothing white sound, the plonk plonk plonk of the thongs, seem to be cleaning out Phil's week-cluttered brain cells as they clean away the grit of the road.

There are a number of these moments for suburban repose that appear to have been created as a quick fix of quiet for us as we dash around town doing our chores. Inching through the Lethe Brushless Car Wash may be the best example of taking a breath, psychically speaking. No thoughts cluttering our brain. No daydreaming. Not even any praying. Just sitting there as our cerebellums are being scrubbed clean.

Waiting in the car line of a bank's drive-in window sometimes offers the same opportunity. But in this situation there is always the chance that we can be jolted from relaxation to agitation when the driver in front of us takes so long to transact her "No more than three transactions, please" that we'd swear those transactions were (1) establishing a trust fund, (2) securing a mortgage and (3) exchanging a mess of *escudos* for American dollars.

Waiting to pick up a child from her dance lesson or a husband at the train station, waiting for your son as he runs into the store for a gallon of milk ("I'm sorry, Mom, they didn't have any skimmed, I had to get *real* milk") are some other moments that give us a chance for a quick mind sweep.

Phil, having had his head scrubbed clean at the car wash, now drives across town to Patsy's. Phil needs half soles and heels on his brown loafers, Janice needs lifts on a couple of pairs of shoes, and B.J.'s only "good" shoes need some reconstructive stitching.

Patsy has been the community cobbler as long as most residents can remember. In fact, he was fixing shoes in town when people called the shoe repairman a cobbler. Patsy's business success can be documented by the fact that he has had to move three times, first to accommodate new equipment, then to have room for a makeshift discount (very, very discount) shoe salon and, most recently, to have enough shelf space to store the dozens upon dozens of pairs of shoes that come in every week for repair and revitalization.

As distressed as Phil can be about some people's chosen occupations, distressed enough to lapse into Uppity Pity, he views Patsy and his line of work as something positive and serene and bordering on the noble. Patsy the person has something to do with Phil's opinion of shoe repairing as a profession. Patsy is always upbeat, even when he has to tell an anxious and annoyed customer that it will be impossible to have her shoes ready next week, his being "backed up all the way to the wall the way I am."

In Phil's estimation, Patsy cares for his craft—and it shows. He sees Patsy sitting hunched over his work station, slicing pieces of excess rubber from a heel so it will be perfect. He hears Patsy ask a customer to wait a few extra minutes so he can polish and buff the newly repaired shoes. He sees Patsy toss a pair of laces into the brown bag, saying . . . "No charge . . . you gonna need 'em soon . . . the old ones gonna snap on you any minute."

Patsy's pride shows. And it smells, too.

Some people walk into Patsy's and get a whiff of leather, polish, and that singular odor produced by the friction of soles and heels being rounded and smoothed on the lathe. Phil notices those smells too, but he senses another bouquet in Patsy's shop: the smell of *good*.

There are places whose smells transcend their actual aromas and what they are meant to represent. These are places whose odors besmell a higher olfactory calling. Patsy's place is one. It's not merely redolent of wax and leather, but of . . . *good*. And Aunt Alice's kitchen isn't filled only with the fragrance of fresh banana nut bread and hot cocoa, but of . . . *good*. And when she was younger, Jennifer's room didn't just smell of that marvelous blend of Bubble Yum and shampoo and talcum, but of . . . *good*.

> I have always thought, as You have known,
> That my nose was too long and pointed.
> (Although I'm curious to know what they'd say)

I've refrained from asking people
What they actually think of my nose.

Yet maybe, just maybe
My nose's shape and size
Allow me to be more attuned
To those smells that reflect
The goodness of people
Doing Your will
And loving every minute of it.

Doing *any*body's will isn't easy, whether that anybody is spouse or parent, God or governor. But it is a lot easier, to the point of enjoying and loving the will-doing, when one senses that there is inherent goodness associated with the activity. Which Phil senses, sniffs out actually, as he goes about his Saturday-morning business, the knight errant (knight errand?) that he temporarily is.

The hardware store smells of fertilizer, oil and pine. Where does the pine smell come from? Phil inhales to investigate. The new stepladders leaning against the far wall? The kitty scratching posts? Or from Frank, from Frank himself? The young proprietor, Frank, inherited the store from Ansel, his father. Frank has no concept of time management. He will spend up to a half hour with a customer trying to find the right-size Molly bolt. That's thirty minutes for a dollar-or-so sale. But then again, maybe Frank has a different point of view about time and how it should be spent. Maybe, to Frank's way of thinking, time should be spent on people, not profit. Frank smells of pine . . . and *good.*

Then onto the musty, slightly gaspy smell of the bookstore and its trio of owners: Agnes, Desmond and Cameron. Phil enters, sniffs and sets off in search of the latest Peter DeVries literate lunacy. "If there's one writer who understands, really understands us folks in suburbia, it's DeVries," Phil expostulates to anybody within the sound of his mumbling voice.

"You mean Cheever didn't?" asks Desmond of the keen hearing.

"And Bombeck doesn't?" asks Agnes, similarly gifted.

"Updike neither?" shouts Cameron from the back of the shop, where he is rearranging the Cooking/Health shelves.

"For *my* money," answers Phil, having found the book and now looking at the blurb, ". . . which I see is $17.95 . . . har, har . . . DeVries tells us we shouldn't be ashamed of wearing our hearts and our heartbreaks on our sleeves. He tells us we can brood openly . . . and we can speak of our passions and our relationships with a kind of disarming candor. He tells us we can . . ."

"Ooooo, heavy!" shouts Cameron, now having moved on to the Children/Teens shelves.

"What a fan! What a devotee!" says Agnes.

"I suppose Cheever could have been considered by some as being somewhat superficial," says Desmond, curling up both lips in a moue of agreement.

Phil wonders what it is, the smell of books, the rows of volumes of, pages of, supposed knowledge that gets him to wax ecstatic about a popular, but hardly very heady, commercial novelist?

Ecstatic?

Or is he being pretentious?

Absurd?

Come on, Phil. Get off it. It's Saturday morning. You're in a local bookstore, a neighborhood bookstore, not in a sophomore English lit class. Where do you come off pontificating like a fatuous book reviewer? And on Saturday morning?

Yes, it *is* Saturday morning, when little blue Smurfs are skipping across the TV screen la-la-ing their way through another adventure, when lions of industry are roaring as they flail away in deep and impossible sand traps, when families are lugging useless artifacts onto their front lawns in the hope of convincing some passing souls that their discarded junk is the bargain of a lifetime. It's Saturday morning, and with all this community triviality, there's Phil in the bookstore carrying on like a pedantic jerk.

Phil has had to battle pretentiousness constantly. Pretentiousness is a malaise that suburbia is especially prone to. (And malaise is a pretentious word that we suburbanites are also frequently prone to.) But there may be an excuse (some may read it as a rationalization) for our pretentiousness. We have a sense of pride in our environs, such an overwhelming sense of pride in our suburbs, that we sometimes feel we are special because of them. We assume a persona (whoops, another pretentious word) we really don't have a right to, nor do we really want it; still, we find ourselves sliding into some suburbanly inspired, unjustified role.

Phil has no intention of passing himself off as a civic sociologist or a doctor of suburban cultural studies, yet there he is being banally bookish simply because he's browsing through the village bookstore. "This isn't Oxford, for crying out loud, Phil, this is your little town bookstore. Hmmmm? It must be the smell," thinks Phil, catching himself in mid-airs while he is putting them on.

Airs, however, are virtually impossible to put on as one leans back, legs fully outstretched, mouth wide open. That's the position in which Phil finds himself as his Saturday morning grinds down. Quite literally grinds down.

Phil is in the dentist's chair. There's nothing seriously wrong with his teeth. Just the regular six-month cosmetic correction, the abrading away of yellow to reveal those pristine pearly whites.

Unlike so many others, Phil has never found the dentist's chair especially threatening. Nor has he found the dentist especially threatening either. Especially *his* dentist. Herbert Spellman, D.M.D., is a tall, spindly man whose bonily thin arms seem a part of the robotic dental equipment in his office. Dr. Spellman's lankiness helps fuel one of Phil's dentist-chair fantasies, a childish one. He envisions Herb (Dentists and doctors enjoy a first-name relationship with their suburban patients. Or do they? Do they really enjoy it, or would they rather be called by their professional appellations?) as his Spockish galactic companion traveling through space with him.

No, Phil's fantasy hasn't been induced by an injection or a topically applied painkiller. It's the chair. Phil has always found the dentist's chair to be a sort of contoured conveyance. It takes him away, for an hour or so, to the darnedest places. Some of those daydreaming destinations are exotic; e.g., outer space, the Masters Golf Tournament (where Phil sinks a thirty-foot putt on the final hole to win the championship and the green jacket), and a nightclub in Las Vegas where Frank Sinatra introduces Phil as the one singer in the world that he had hoped to be as good as. But if a man flirting with middle age can sit in a dentist's chair and fantasize about a singing engagement at Caesar's Palace, he can also rinse his mouth of that minty abrasive and fantasize about eternity:

> You know I'm not one for crowds, God,
> And the psychological tests show
> I work much better alone
> Than I do in a group.
> So You can appreciate, I hope,
> My concern about eternity.
> Which concern?

> *This* concern:
> With the billions of souls
> You've already welcomed to Forever,
> How, God, how
> Can someone who always loved solitude
> Ever feel comfortable in all that
> Joyful congestion?

But all of Phil's dentist's-chair fantasies are not divinely or Walter Mittily inspired. Phil's thoughts about an overpopulated heaven head to a thought about a small office, this small office, occupied for eight hours or more each day by a solitary man and a solitary woman.

"Talk about intimacy! How does Herb get through the day with just Julia around, with just he and his hygienist in this little office alone together for hours on end? How can someone work so close to a woman and not feel an occasional . . . every once in a while . . . an urge, a yen, whatever? What's intimacy, anyway? Isn't it closeness? Physical and spiritual closeness? I mean, there they are each with their fingers in my mouth at the same time. Now, that's intimacy. When do even a husband and a wife ever have that kind of intimacy? Fingers in the mouth of a stranger, well just about a stranger, at the same time? Herb with his tooth buffer, or whatever is the name of that tooth polisher, and Julia with the suction tube that's vacuuming up all the water and blood. It's weird, yes, but it's intimate. I mean, much more intimate than a work situation with a guy and his secretary. That relationship's nowhere near as close as this one. The two of them hunching over me and surrounding, probing this third party and. . . ." Phil winces at the crass course his fantasizing is taking.

Herb reads the wince as pain. Herb never calls pain, pain. "Are you experiencing some discomfort, Phil?"

"Nargh. Nargh. I'hm fahne. Just fahne."

Phil can't really tell the dentist that he *is* experiencing some discomfort, because then he would have to explain the kind of discomfort he is experiencing. No, he can't tell the dentist. But he can tell God:

> I thought I had this sleazy quirk licked,
> This habit of describing relationships
> (Anything from romantic to raunchy)
> That exist only in my imagination.
> But here I go again.

And here I *am* again,
Asking You, not to explain *why* I do it
(Which is shrinks' work, not God's),
But praying that You allow me to see people
Only as they are
Or as they want to be,
Not as I demeaningly dream them to be.
Amen.

SATURDAY AFTERNOON

Running in the Family. Catching in the Family.
Sliding, Jumping and Diving in the Family.

A suburb, for better or worse, fosters a sense of community the way a city simply cannot. For worse? When is it for worse? When the suburb becomes, intentionally or unintentionally, insular, and wraps itself up in its own lush fescue and dense dark green pachysandra.

And for better? When the suburb presents itself to itself as A Playground for the Human Spirit. Since the human spirit needs and feeds on affection, recognition, and continuity, there must be contrivances that nurture the spirit's cravings. Contrivance need not be an unpleasant word. Contrivance's first meaning has nothing to do with deviousness but, rather, with cleverness.

One such clever contrivance is the Community Fair. Once a year, most often toward the shank of the summer, the entire village is invited to participate in a daylong program that includes competition (much of it between families and specific members of families), eating, kid stuff and general bonhomie. (Wasn't he a commander in the French and Indian Wars?)

The day is billed as a "once-a-year community happening."

And what happens?

Any number of things. Swimming events, a scavenger hunt that sends people scurrying and ferreting all over town, a two-and-a-half-mile "fun" (?) run, a crazy-costume contest, dunking the village manager, throwing pies at the school-board members, a beautiful-baby contest, all sorts of races and contests and endurance tests that reward people who stayed away from the sausage-and-peppers booth until the games are over and severely punish those who eat before they compete.

By the end of his superweek of creation, had God fashioned a community, he undoubtedly would have also created a Community Day right there and then. But, alas, two do not a community make, even though the two are as fun-loving a duo as Adam and Eve. So God had to wait a few millennia before He suggested Community Day to some suburban officeholders who immediately saw the merit of His idea, although they may have inadvertently neglected to attribute the idea to Him.

Rather than take you through the entire Community Day schedule (the Mother-and-Son-Under-Twelve Hundred-Yard Butterfly Relay is an event even *Sports Illustrated* would be hard-pressed to describe), let me highlight two contests that, perhaps better than any other, portray the fragile goodness of suburbia.

Fragile?

Yes. In the sense that a piece of bone china is fragile. The human spirit, especially in a communal situation, must be treated as carefully, even caressingly, as a bone-china teacup. And just as respectfully. Gingerly, in fact. And like that piece of bone china, the human spirit is also a source of admiration, a thing of beauty. Fragile *and* utilitarian. Admirable, but not intended to be gawked at from the other side of a cabinet glass. No. Both china and the spirit are meant to be celebrated and used.

The first example of fragile goodness is built around that most fragile of objects: the egg. The Community Day Husband and Wife Egg Toss, perhaps a more relevant life-link than the semiprecious-bone-china allusion, provides a surrealistic scenario worthy of Buñuel or Fellini:

Between twenty and thirty couples, in various stages of marital longevity, participate in the event. Wife and husband face each other three feet apart. There is no single line of wives facing a line of husbands. Each pair of partners may choose whichever orientation they prefer. The event is held at high noon, so there is no "sun field" to blind one or the other.

The event is played by tossing a raw egg from one partner to another without, obviously, breaking the henfruit. At three feet this is hardly a feat. Ah, but with each successful toss both thrower and catcher must take a step backward before the next heave. And so it goes—toss, catch, step backward, toss, catch, step backward, until only one couple remains with their egg intact. This can mean that contestant couples may be as much as thirty or more feet apart at the conclusion of the event.

Now, how is the human spirit elevated by tossing an egg from wife to husband, from husband to wife?

Well, in those few minutes it takes to play out the game, the dialogue between spouses provides a splendid example of what wonders loving, helpful communication can achieve. Although, earlier that day, wife might have snapped at husband for not replacing the burned-out range-hood light all week long, and husband might have passed a sarcastic remark about her dried-out, over-microwaved bacon, their language on the egg-toss field is one of caring. Caring, with just a touch of sensuality tossed in.

Listen.

She (tossing):
"Oooo . . . careful."

        He (catching): "Nice flip. Nice and easy."

He (tossing):
"Soft hands now . . .
gotta have soft hands."

        She (catching): "Say . . . that sort of floated in."

She (tossing):
"What does soft
hands' mean?"

        He (catching): "You have to catch it on the fleshy tips of your fingers . . . and then let your hands sort of fall away."

He (tossing):
"Watch it, honey.
Bend from the waist.
Move with the egg."

        She (catching): "Move with the egg? That's . . . that's . . . got it! . . . that's hilarious. You know, you're hilarious sometimes, sweetie, and . . ."

She (tossing)
". . . will you look at
that? Only three
couples left . . . here
goes."

> *He* (catching): "Yarrgh! A little higher
> next time. Wait'll I get the dandelions
> out of my teeth, hon."

He (tossing):
"Cup your hands now . . .
this is a long one . . .
cup your hands."

> *She* (catching): "Got it. I got it. Right
> on the old fleshy tips!"

Now, this quite apparently is not Elizabeth Barrett and Robert Browning versifying their affection to one another. And no one is about to mistake that dialogue for Cavalier poet material. But there is a youthful exuberance, a genuine caring running through the egg-toss conversation that says something about the human spirit and this particular social contrivance and especially about the particular husband and wife who, incidentally, having realized they've won the contest rush into each other's arms, hug, kiss, and congratulate—and, of course, crush the egg in the process.

The other event at Community Day that can be considered a spiritual classic is the softball game, eighteen people of various shapes, ages, and abilities trying to do things they once could or recently saw someone doing on TV. Eighteen people. Two teams of nine, right? Wrong. Not in Community Day softball. Eighteen people on each side!

Originally the overpopulated diamond was in response to the clamor created by so many people who wanted to play Community Day ball, many more than Doubleday's rules could accommodate. So it was decided to augment the prescribed nine. The augmentation varied from year to year until finally it was determined that eighteen was the most the playing field could accommodate: five infielders, four short-fielders, six outfielders, the pitcher, the catcher and a catcher to back up the catcher.

The squad that takes the field looks like a collection of models for some latter-day Norman Rockwell. Their ages range from seven to the mid-sixties, and perhaps one gentleman has reached seventy. Shapes have an even wider range, from the prodigiously bellied to the tautly muscled, from a svelte teenage girl to a mother of five whose hips and thighs disguise her quickness. Yes, Community Day softball is for all sexes. And for all abilities, too, as the game glaringly, unsparingly reveals.

In the first two innings the hotshots among the eclectic eighteen leap and dive and give notice that they are young and vital and indestructible. Since the field is so crowded, the hotshots have to be careful not to leap and dive into their teammates, most of whom are *not* indestructible.

In the third and fourth innings, the spotlight turns away from the sprawling, tumbling athletes to the unlikely, one-day-a-year ballplayers. Prodigiously Bellied, playing short field on the right side, reacting to a screaming line drive over his head, doesn't move an inch but sticks his gloved arm up in a "Hail, Caesar" gesture and, "thwomp," the ball buries itself deep into his glove. Teammates cheer. Spectators laugh.

Mother of Five, after singling, decides to go from first to third on another single. The throw is there in time to beat her, but with a slide she'll remember—and feel—for days, Mother of Five kicks the ball out of the third baseperson's glove and is safe.

The Back-Up Catcher, a corporate hustler as well as Community Day dynamo, chases a high foul ball into the soda concession stand, sending himself and seven assorted flavors, including diet and no-caffeine brands, flying.

One of the many joys of playing as a member of an eighteen-person team is that you can stand unmolested and untested in left center field and observe the human hilarity unfolding before you. That observation might even lead to a commentary/chat:

> If we can join with one another
> For two or three hours,
> Not teasing, but treasuring
> Each other's shortcomings,
> Why can't we stretch out the treasuring
> For weeks and months at a time?
>
> If we're able to react
> To little goofs and gaffes
> With jokes and smiles

And good-natured laughs,
Why can't all that humility
Be enough to bind all humanity
In perpetual mutual respect?

As the game heads to its conclusion and the sun heads for the horizon, Keystone Kop-like rundowns, a triple play, outfield near-collisions, and some of the strangest batting stances since Mel Ott and Sadaharu Oh keep the spectators as involved in the game as the players are. Sometimes more so.

The sun, however, slips behind the horizon before the bottom of the ninth can be completed. To be more precise, before even the bottom of the seventh can be completed.

The ball game and most of its runs, hits and hilarious errors will soon fade from the memory of both the game's participants and its onlookers. In a week everyone will even have forgotten which team was ahead when the game was called. Still, for much longer than a couple of weeks or a month, certain players will be spoken of as local mini-legends because of some bit of humanity they flashed during the game.

Mother of Five, for example, will be known as "Spikes" as long as she lives in the community. No, she wasn't wearing spikes, she was wearing tennis shoes, when she slid into the bag, loosening the ball from the third-sacker's glove, but somebody in the stands yelled, "How to go! How to go! Spikes high! Keep those spikes high."

The woman who had been known for her entire life as Mary Catherine—and only as Mary Catherine—will now be called, and almost always so, "Spikes." Unkind? Rude? Not at all. The name "Spikes" is a warm and loving recognition of a person who, for a few seconds, rewarded her fellow human beings.

Rewarded?

Yes, exactly the same way sports and film and music stars reward their fellow human beings. Oh, the people might not know they're doing that. They may not have programmed themselves in a rewarding mode when they took the field. Whether it's the Community Day softball game or the World Series, it's not likely that participants trot out onto the field saying to themselves, "Okay, team, let's reward the crowd, ourselves, and every last person."

But that's what the spectators, deep down, expect. In just about every sort of situation and place, we yearn for people to elevate us, elevate us and our very existence. That's the reward we look for, without knowing we're looking for it.

We want to revel in the musical talent of "The Boss." We want to cheer the exploits of "The Refrigerator," and on a different life stage, but no less significant, we want to rejoice that "Spikes" (née Mary Catherine, a.k.a. Mother of Five) can slide at her age and station in life, can kick the ball out of a defensive player's hand, can finish the game with a raw and painful bruise on her thigh and can accept our joking admiration with dignity and aplomb and good cheer.

As can "Baskets." Until that ball game, he was Walter Flanagan, a retired mailman and retired so long ago that he had actually delivered mail on foot to doors, not as mail is delivered in the suburbs today, by van to boxes. Walter was just standing around second base, enjoying the day and the pageantry when pop-up after pop-up was hit his way. Arthritis has made lifting arms above shoulders painful for Walter, so he put out his hands as if holding a basket and pop-up after pop-up plopped easily into Walter's hands.

But Walter no more. He's "Baskets" Flanagan now, enshrined in village memory because of a wonderful selfish communal reason: his actions elevated us, all of us, made us all seem a little more important, because Walter, er, "Baskets" became a little more important to us.

SATURDAY NIGHT

The Charity—But Just How Much Charity?—Ball

If the most recent day-parts of the week appear to have assumed a rather heavy social emphasis, there's a reason for it. This part of the suburban week actually is a nonstop social whirl more often than not. Beginning with Friday night and quite frequently going straight through Sunday night, the burbs bustle with one social activity after another. With all the possibilities however, neither a tailgate party at a prep school nor a local celebrity auction nor a clambake on a neighbor's new flagstone terrace can hold a chi-chi candle to the Saturday Night Charity Ball.

Depending on the time of year, the Charity Ball may be known as The Spring Fling, The Fall Frolic or The Snowball. There don't seem to be many, if any, balls in the summer, maybe because no one's been able to come up with a cute and clever name for one.

Phil and Janice have averaged about 2.4 formal suburban events a year, the Charity Ball being the gussiest of them. Phil professes to dislike going to them. He always grouses, but, an hour into the affair, he has totally forgotten what he doesn't like about it and is in the running for that night's Life of the Party. Janice always looks forward to these dressy dances with youthful anticipation.

Occasionally she shares her sense of anticipation:

> I'm decades past my junior prom,
> But You know that, don't You, God?

Yet here I am still getting excited
By another dressy night out.
Oh, it's not a teenage giddiness, no,
But a sort of grown-up gaiety,
Tempered, of course,
By those ageless questions:
"Is my hair too poufy?"
"Am I wearing too much jewelry?"
"Am I showing too much cleavage?"

The first dance of the evening is danced without the accompaniment of music. The band hasn't even begun to set up yet. The only accompaniment for the first dance is the tinkle of ice cubes.

The first dance is danced at the cocktail reception. This is a time for people to slide, two-step, even dip from one conversation to another. Many years ago, in his book *Power,* Michael Korda charted how to move slickly from chat to chat at a cocktail party. Korda showed how to rotate around the center of the room, yet always be able to edge into any of the "power corners" should that seem the politically savvy thing to do.

God, eternity's most extraordinary eavesdropper, picks up and processes all those bytes of conversation at the Charity Ball cocktail reception. God's creatures move, form clusters, separate and reunite. As they do so, they sip, smile and say to each other:

> "She's been accepted
> at Georgetown, Ham-
> ilton and the Univer-
> sity of Virginia, but
> she really wants to
> go to Princeton."

"You can imagine
how upset we were.
Toxoplasmosis
sounds so dreadful."
  "I can
  imagine."
"But *can* you?
Can you really?"

"Harry refuses to
wear one."
  "You bet I do. You
  have to be as skinny
  as Manute Bol to look
  good in a cummerbund."
"Who's Manute Bol?"

"I've been drinking
red, rather than white,
lately."
    "They say
    that's a trend."
"Am I in the vanguard
or the rear guard of it?"

"Look."
  "Where?"
"Don't look now."   "Can you tell
  "Why?"   the difference
"They're looking."   between somebody
  "Who?"   who's on drugs
"It's okay to look   and somebody
now."   who's depressed?"
    "Where?"
                                     "Er . . . why . . . do
                                     you ask?"

        "Heisman, Schmeisman, the kid can't run."
                    "Who has to run
                    with an arm like
                    that?"
        "You think an arm is enough for a pro career?"
                    "Sometimes a
                    mouth is enough."
                                "Yeah, come to think
                                of it, that's all *I*
                                ever needed."
        "I would have sworn they'd
        be accepted into The Club.
        I couldn't see any . . . what
        do you call them?"
                "Impediments?"
        "Right, I couldn't see any
        impediments."
                "What does he
                do for a living?"
        "He's in arbitrage."
                "There's your "impediment."

"Damascus is not
in Iraq, it's in
Iran."
 "It is not.
 That's where
 all those
 clandestine
 meetings are . . ."
  "Pardon me, I couldn't help
  overhearing, but Damascus
  is in Syria."
"Yes, well, thank
you, but we
weren't talking
about *that*
Damascus."
  "Not *that* Damascus?
  There's another one?"
 "Is there
 just one
 Portland?"
  "Um . . . well . . . no . . .
  er . . . excuse me . . .
  must find my table."

                              "I didn't date till I was 18."
                                "I was in college."
                              "What do you call a date?"
                                "When you're alone. One on one.
                                Not in a group."
                              "Do you consider tonight a date?"

"Menlo Park was where *Edison*
worked, not Marconi."
  "Where did Marconi
  work?"   "Chervil isn't
"Somewhere just off Mulberry   anything like
Street, I think."   lovage."
                                                 "IT ISN'T?"

The bell sounds for dinner, but the dancedrinkers don't seem anxious for the cocktail hour to end. They continue to circle. People slink out of one cluster and sidle into another. They discuss everything from the emigration of Senegalese to the United States to what variety of mustard you should use when making honey mustard dressing.

The bell sounds again, more insistently this time, and Janice, turning toward the room, let's out a bit of a barely audible gasp and says to her circle of chatmates, "The swan is sweating early tonight."

Nowhere, absolutely nowhere, not in Ian Fleming or John le Carré or in Robert Ludlum will you find as mysterious, as cloak-and-dagger-cryptic a line as that. "The swan is sweating early tonight." So deep. So enigmatic. Whatever could it mean? A secret code? Could it mean that Janice is some sort of suburban operative?

No, just observant.

Chef Julio's ice-sculpture swan is melting. The evening has barely begun and the ice swan is melting. Perhaps the room is too hot, or the decorative piece had been improperly frozen. Whatever the case, Janice has noticed it and feels compelled to inform her friends of that fact in a rather poetic fashion. As they stroll into the dining room, Janice also decides to inform her Friend and Neighbor, who, she feels:

> Seeing the swan fading
> In the party's very first hour,
> Reminds me to ask You, God,
> For the staying power
> To remain charming and calm
> When it gets loud and late,
> A couple of conditions
> Of sound and time
> That, as we all know,
> I have trouble
> Dealing with.
> Amen.

Late hours and loud noise may present problems for Janice, but one of the things she does not have trouble dealing with is new people. Janice has long been considered a potential candidate for public office because of her ability to meet new people and have the new people feel good about having been met.

Feeling good about having been met?

Yes. How many times have we stood in reception lines and been introduced to people who we felt couldn't care less who we were and why we were even there? Or maybe we've been at the other end of the handshake, giving our guests a "Hello, glad to see you" with little or no visible, audible or tangible gladness in our voice, handshake or heart.

Later in the evening, in the ladies' room, one of Janice's tablemates will say to her, "Janice, I don't know how you do it. You're so good with foreigners." The word "foreigners," as spoken by the woman sharing Janice's ladies' room mirror, sounds more ominous than its synonym, "aliens," were it to have been spoken by some space-movie earthling.

For many of us suburban earthlings, the influx of foreigners into our leafy, compost-heapy loveliness does indeed create problems. Not racial problems. Social ones. Not problems of hue or venue, but problems of communication.

Since the world has become, at least to the media, a global village (what a fascinating phrase . . . "village" has such country and suburban connotations, rather than the expansive connotation that global has . . . is global village our latest oxymoron?) Belgians and Japanese and Saudi Arabians are bedding down in the same American bedroom communities as natives of Massachusetts and Ohio and Oregon are. And since, as we have maintained, the suburbs are parochial, albeit green and parochial, pastures, there is a chilliness with which many of the international transplants are greeted (not quite the word), welcomed (not the right word), confronted (that's more like it).

Yet it's a chill that stems not from disdain, but from discomfort. We may be suburban (that's been acknowledged) and sophisticated (that can be alleged) and intelligent (that's up for debate), but when it comes to communicating with new residents from the Old World, we squirm. And while we're squirming we say things to each other like:

"I'd like to get to know her, but I just can't understand a word Miyako says."

"Sure we can invite the Castillos over for dinner, but what in the world will we talk about? We've been to Barcelona only once—and then only for a day, and the cathedral was closed. So what would we have to talk about?"

"If he were an Italian who liked soccer, that's one thing. But he's an Italian egghead. I don't know anything about modern Italian novelists."

Disdain? No.

Discomfort? Absolutely.

A Foreign Couple is seated at Phil and Janice's table because there are two empty places there. The Foreign Couple did not come with a "party," the phrase that signifies belonging, as in "Oh, you're with the Jensen party!" The Foreign Couple is, therefore, directed to any table where there are two free seats, as there are at Phil and Janice's table.

Janice speaks no foreign language. But she asks Universal Questions. Anyone who asks Universal Questions can be comfortable in almost any situation. And similarly, anyone who has Universal Questions asked of himself feels welcome, at ease, and happy to have been met.

Janice asks the Foreign Lady some Universal Questions and breaks the ice.

"Do you have a garden back home? What do you grow?"

"Have you traveled extensively? Where have you been?

"Do you drive?"

"What do you think of our music?"

And then comes the most popular Universal Question of them all, the one question that almost guarantees comfort and pleasant conversation for the rest of the evening—and sometimes beyond that. That Universal Question: "Do you have any children?"

Throughout Janice's cheerful interrogation, Phil is at the other end of the table being his outgoing self. He always is. He is outgoing at dinner. He was outgoing during drinks. But he is *not* outgoing on the dance floor. In fact, Phil tries to arrange his ball evening so that he will never have to go out onto the dance floor. When certain numbers are played that might conceivably call for his participation on the dance floor, he usually excuses himself for the men's room, a phone call or a freshening of his drink. So, when Janice says to Phil, in a voice loud enough to be heard over the band's first few bars of The Bunny Hop, "Phil, how about introducing Elena to American dancing?" his jaw drops—and from the resultant open mouth comes the sound "Whuh?"

Leading half of the Foreign Couple onto the dance floor, Phil turns back to Janice, rolls his eyes, puffs out his cheek and wrinkles his nose, a barrage of facial expressions that add up to "HOW COULD YOU DO THIS TO ME?"

To Elena, Phil says, "Do you like to dance?"

Elena replies, "Yes. When I was a girl I was a folk dancer with a big dance group."

"Oh."

"Yes, I like to dance very much."

"That's nice. Uh, well, you see many people in this country consider this dance . . . the Bunny Hop . . . to be America's most popular . . . America's favorite folk dance."

And as Phil places his hands on Elena's hips, he says to God:

> Why do You think she did this to me?
> She knows I don't like to dance.
> Sure, I probably should have been
> Paying more attention
> To those people
> Than I was,
> But dragging me into her conversation
> Would have been much nicer
> Than being dragged
> Onto the dance floor.

At the same time, Janice is saying to God:

> Why did I do that?
> To be cute?
> To cut off his conversation
> At the other end of the table?
> Or to take him away from his drink?
> I probably could have found
> A better way,
> And if not better,
> Certainly kinder.
> Then why, do You suppose,
> I didn't?

Janice and Phil will replay the evening over their 2 A.M. ginger ales. They had found, some time back, that the carbonation of the drink and the bite of the ginger were a more refreshing way to end a long evening than the traditional warm milk. Sipping while slipping out of their evening wear, husband and wife will recount snippets of conversations conversed, funny things said, strange things worn, insights gleaned, new acquaintances made, former neighbors revisited, and yes, the Bunny Hop.

"I'm sorry, Phil . . . I don't know why I . . ."

"She's a folk dancer. Did you know that? Elena's a folk dancer."

"Really?"

"Well, she was one back there. Danced with a troupe, a big group."

"You mean you danced with a *professional* dancer?"

"C'mon, don't kid me."

"See, you're really not bad. You'd be pretty doggone good, a better-than-average dancer, if you'd just get out there more often."

"You really think so?

"I *know* so."

"I wonder."

"You wonder what?"

"I wonder, now that I've mastered The Bunny Hop, you think I'm ready for the tango?"

Tossing a pillow (medium firm) at him, Janice says, "Good night, Phil."

"Good night, honey."

SUNDAY MORNING

The Definite Article

And that's exactly what Sunday morning is: the definite article. But definitely.

The family eagerly awaits THE doughnuts to arrive. "When did Daddy go out for THE doughnuts? He's still not back."

And the family anxiously looks for THE paper. Every five minutes or so, somebody goes out to look on the front porch. "It's almost nine-thirty. Hasn't THE paper come yet?"

And after THE paper and THE doughnuts have been devoured on Sunday morning, it will be time to call THE relatives.

Yes, Sunday morning is the definite article.

Now, the reason Daddy hasn't returned with the doughnuts yet is that he has been gathering information. More inconsequential, nonseismic information is passed along on Sunday morning than during any other day-part of the week.

Think about it: The reason the family is edgy waiting for the paper is that, depending on their favorite interests, various members will want to read the late sport scores, the gossip columns, the record and movie reviews, and maybe even the headlines. All that is information.

And after Sunday services, worshipers will gather outside the house of worship not to review the rite just performed, but to review the community highlights and lowlights of the week just past. On the golf course, at the gas station, wherever people gather on Sunday morning, they gather information.

With all these data sources, there is one Sunday news source to beat all others. It just may be the most definitive font of what's-happening-in-town. It just may be the ultimate unimpeachable authority for who's-making-news. And what is this source of information?

The bakery.

The bakery?

Well, more accurately, one special section of the bakery: the custom-made-cakes section.

By standing and reading the icing on the custom-baked cakes, a curious suburbanite can learn just about everything his village and certain villagers are up to. While other patrons are queued up for their Danishes and crumb buns and raspberry meltaways, the seriously snoopy soul will press his inquisitive nose to the window of the bakery's decorated-cakes case. And there will be the news of the day.

"Happy Birthday to Tony" reads a precisely iced white-and-blue-flowered beauty. The cake's size indicates that Tony, lucky fellow, has a host of friends. No skimpy six-slice cake this. This is a biggie. And since no age is indicated either by the icing or a plastic number, one can assume that Tony is somewhere in midlife. How so? Well, middle-agers don't broadcast their age. Youngsters flaunt their youth. The elderly like to boast of their longevity. There are two or three decades in between that people don't care to ballyhoo.

Yet, right next to Tony's cake is, indeed, a cake that boasts of longevity. It, too, is a big cake. And the icing/writing reads, "Happy 80th Birthday John." The assumption that a canny cake reader will make is that the greeting is being proffered the senior celebrant by friends, rather than family. Why that conclusion? If it were family, chances are the greeting would read, "Happy Birthday Dad" or "Happy Birthday Gramps." No, the straight, simple "John" gives away its author and the cake's donor as being a friend, and not a relative, of the new octogenarian.

Friends are also feting Diane, apparently enceinte, since the lady is being wished "A Shower of Happiness." No, not a wedding shower, since the yellow high-caloric frosting flowers are accented by a pair of diaper pins imbedded in the icing, a graphic reminder of the drudgery that will follow the joy.

Two Sunday cake-case findings are items for the religious pages. In each case, the bold use of two names, rather than one, tell the reader that these tortes of tribute are for postbaptismal celebrations.

"God Bless Amanda Marie."

"God Bless Paul Vincent."

Red letters on a field of white icing. Must the icing always be white? To signify purity? Or just for legibility?

Much more difficult to understand, maddeningly so even for the most seasoned of Sunday-morning cake readers, is a weighty number that says, "Best Wishes to Stacy and Walter." What makes this cake especially puzzling is the number "17" in thick chocolate icing.

What does it mean? What's the story? Are Stacy and Walter twin sister and brother concelebrating their seventeenth birthday? Or are they an unrelated twosome being feted at a common birthday party thrown by a bunch of thoughtful, and frugal, friends? If either possibility is correct, then why not say, "Happy Birthday," on the cake? Why "Best Wishes"?

Or if Stacy and Walter happen to be wife and husband, why not wish them, with no chance of misinterpretation, "Happy Anniversary"?

But might the number stand for something other than years married or years alive? How about the number of years at the same firm? Strange to celebrate a seventeenth year, though. And that's not the kind of thing to whoop about on a Sunday. Not when America is at home and not at work.

How about this? The number 17 is the number of Stacy and Walter's new home . . . they've just bought a house on Blueberry Lane . . . *17* Blueberry Lane. Possible. Yes, it's possible, but something of a stretch. A romantic stretch, though, thinking someone might present a decorated cake to a couple moving into their new home.

More and more people are becoming aware of this new news source, and this may soon create certain difficulties. Imagine the jockeying and the elbowing that might take place as people try to be the first in town to learn about Tony and Diane and Amanda Marie. Rather than line up for their customary croissants, people might flock to the cake case, craning their necks to get a peek at the morning headlines, jostling one another in the ribs as they attempt to move closer to get a look at all the news that's fit to ice. Not only would that kind of scene cause the bakeshop proprietors a certain amount of justified consternation (the very best kind of consternation there is), but some of the celebrants might also consider it an invasion of privacy.

Maybe some of the people being feted and presented cakes to commemorate such and such an occasion would rather not have the occasion publicly known. They might be very concerned about prying cake readers at the bakery. Who knows? They might even ask to have their cakes specially iced to read, "Happy Birthday, Anon." and "God Bless Occupant."

At any rate, although a fancifully decorated cake makes for a festive Sunday celebration, all such events need not be accompanied by a mocha-lined, multilayered creation slathered with vanilla butter cream. Not at all. No, a half dozen jelly doughnuts, two glazed; one long cruller; and a plain cinnamon doughnut can be considered celebration fare just as well. In fact, what the people eating those doughnuts are celebrating may be more important than a birthday or an anniversary.

When a suburban family gathers around a platter of doughnuts (remember when they used to be called "sinkers"?) on Sunday morning, it could be celebrating togetherness, memories, or pajamas—or, under some circumstances, all three.

Togetherness. Sunday morning is one of the few times of the week when a family quorum may be present. Sleep-overs may cause one child to be away, but then again, when the sleep-over is at *your* house, the child count may be augmented by five or six, which, in turn, will increase the attendant doughnut requirement exponentially.

Since everyone in the house does not bolt out of bed at the same time on Sunday morning, total Togetherness may take a little time to achieve. Sooner or later, however, the kitchen will be filled with people in various stages of alertness or fogginess. These people have one thing in common: they are family.

And in that family may be a person, jelly clinging to his mustache, who is absolutely tickled with the scene that he's a part of. He is so delighted, in fact, that he feels like mindshouting his joy to God:

> Counselors and how-to books
> Say the only way
> For families to thrive—
> Or even survive—
> Is for everyone to be
> "Up front with each other,"
> "Let it all hang out,"
> "Tell it like it is."

The only way?
Is that the only way?
I don't know, God.
I don't know—
And I don't think so.
Our mouths, at this moment,
Are too full to
"tell it like it is,"
But without a word being spoken,
This family,
Right now,
Is together
And at peace.
And I thank You,
O God, how I thank You!

Memories. Doughnuts at breakfast on a Sunday morning, especially if the morning is frosty and it takes five minutes for the windshield to defrost, will remind Daddy, as he drives to the bakery, of *his* daddy. "Couple of sinkers and a strong cup of coffee . . . no finer breakfast has been created or conceived." Thus spake Daddy's daddy when today's head of the household was yesterday's little dickens.

Before jewelry biggies and James Bond determined that "diamonds are forever," someone (oh, Him again?) had determined that "doughnuts are for a long, long time." It's a rare family in which someone doesn't recall a relative bringing back a grease-stained paper bag of stick-to-your-ribs doughnuts, or better still, of a kitchen smelling of and spattered with doughnuts in the making.

Sunday morning is for celebrating memories. Suburbanites not born here remember city doughnut shops where they went with their dads years ago, those fathers who had determined that their children would have a better life—that being translated into a college education, which, sooner or later, leads to a home in the suburbs. Scratch the expression "bringing home the bacon." Every wage earner, it seems, on every Sunday morning brought home the doughnuts. That should have become the expression: "bringing home the doughnuts."

And later, when Dad of blessed memory became Gramps, doughnuts were diagnosed as not being good for him. They were too heavy, too fatty, too greasy for a man with a heart condition. One poached egg (no salt) and dry rye toast had replaced the heavy, thick, richly cinnamoned doughnut. The son of Dad/Gramps remembers this as he sinks his teeth into a sweet glazed doughnut, and he stifles a sigh.

This sigh, as so many sighs often do, becomes a prayer:

> Whenever I was exhorted
> To hold onto the past,
> In classrooms and living rooms,
> In school and at home,
> No one, as I remember,
> Said that I could hold onto
> That precious past
> With my lips
> And my mouth
> And my teeth!
> Yet I am doing just that,
> As I sniffle reminiscences
> Of a man I loved,
> Biting into my doughnut
> And thanking You for the memory
> Of that dear, delightful man.
> Oh, yes,
> And thanks for this appetite
> To remember him by.

Pajamas. One can compare the celebrations of Togetherness and Memories that occur on Sunday mornings in the suburbs with similar celebrations that may happen at other times and in other places. But there's one Sunday-morning celebration that simply can't be compared to anything else. That's the celebration of Pajamas. Actually it's not just pajamas. It's a ragged nightshirt, a lovely, lacy nightgown, a pair of boxer shorts, an old sweatsuit, whatever sleepwear, stylish or strange, that members of the family had selected for the night just ended. All of these, of course, signify intimacy, the real cause for the celebration that pajamas metaphorically represent.

Crumb-bun crumbs on a pink nightgown and flakes that have fallen off a chocolate doughnut and onto a pair of baggy boxer shorts are not the touches a fashion photographer would look for when shooting, supposedly, a sophisticated suburban domestic scene. But they're there—the crumbs and flakes are certainly there. And so is the cinnamon sugar, ringing the kitchen table. As slippered and loafered feet shuffle off to get another cup of coffee or another glass of milk, the cinnamon sugar crackles underfoot. Not a neat setting? Neatness doesn't count. Not here. Not today. Not at a celebration of Pajamas.

What certainly does count is the abiding intimacy and ease among the disheveled doughnut eaters, what counts is their acceptance of each other's morning appearance: the wild, every-which-way hair, the baggy eyes, the stale breath, and the nightwear that reveals body parts one generally prefers to be hidden, not for decency's sake, but because those parts have taken on a fleshiness that's not all that flattering. That's what this morning's celebration is about.

And yes, it *is* certainly flattering—if someone should pause long enough between chomps of a cruller to reflect upon it—that what we would be mortified to reveal to others, the way we would never allow ourselves to appear in public, we feel completely, familially secure about when we are gathered around the Sunday-morning breakfast table.

Although there remain doughnuts to be eaten and sections of THE paper to be read, someone must slip into streetwear, or throw something over his sleepwear, and walk THE dog.

The question is asked, "Who wants to walk THE dog?"

The replies are inconclusive. They are also unintelligible.

"Grympff."

"Urggll."

"Schmmmms."

"Inna minute. Inna minute. Lemme finish this one story."

THE dog sits at the door, waiting . . . waiting not to be walked, but to walk someone.

It's a bizarre suburban phenomenon. When it first began is uncertain, but the fact of the matter is, *the dogs are walking the people.* There has been some strange reversal of power, a transfer of control between dog neck and man hand. The leash no longer restrains the pooch; it tugs the owner, it guides the holder, it forces the human into a role-switched subservience.

Some Sunday-morning sightings:

Aging Rolf, a German shepherd, drags his robed mistress down the road. He bounds for his special turf, a grassy knoll alongside a heavily traveled road. The robed lady is forced to stand in ankle-deep squishiness as the morning traffic zips and honks past. Rolf barks to call attention to himself and the terry-robed lady he is walking.

A man who is an inveterate and speedy walker *without* a dog is now propelled into a madcap dash by his *three* bulldogs. The yelping troika tumbles down the road with the powerless master almost being dragged along. Fortunately the bulldogs have agreed to go in one single direction so that the attached owner is not rent in three.

An attractive short furry reddish dog (breed unknown) walks haughtily in front of his attractive red-headed owner. The lady behaves properly at her end of the leash, slowing up when the canine commands, then accelerating to a brisker pace at the dog's apparent behest.

A dachshund scoots along with a child attached. Robert Benchley wrote that "dachshunds are ideal dogs for small children, as they are already stretched and pulled to such a length that the child cannot do much harm one way or the other." But how about vice versa? What about when the dachshund stretches and pulls the child? What then?

A Weimaraner steps lively down the road, looking right and left to see if people are stopping to admire his sleek coat. The man the Weimaraner is leading wears a shabby coat and a forlorn look. The Weimaraner is better dressed than his loping leash mate. The Weimaraner is even wearing little red boots to protect his paws from the morning dew.

A man strolling, dogless, through the neighborhood observes what seems to be a new relationship between pets and pet owners. He passes along his observation.

> You created creatures,
> So I've been led to believe,
> For our companionship
> And our amusement.
> But now that the dog
> Has taken on the master's role,
> I'll look for *my* companionship
> Inside a goldfish bowl.

Finally, living up to its reputation as the definite article, Sunday morning is the time of week to get in touch with THE relatives. Phone rates are lower and the pace is slower. There's no need to rush through your conversation. You can take time, plenty of time talking with Uncle Luke, who's recuperating from a prostate operation; or your sister, the intern in a hospital in St. Louis; or, if you can rouse her before noon, your daughter, who's away at a boarding school.

One phone call that is made just about every Sunday, however, may not always provide the light and pleasant kind of chitchat the caller had hoped for. That's the call that Suburban Son makes on Sunday morning to City Mom. City Mom is a widow, retired, and her name implies, committed to the city. Suburban Son has asked her on any number of occasions to come out to the suburbs and live with him and his family.

"It's time, Ma, really, it's time you moved in with us. Your neighborhood is getting pretty rough, you know. Why should you have to worry about safety, your safety and your apartment's safety, at your age?"

"Who's worrying? You're the one who should be worrying . . . big mortgage, and the way I hear taxes are shooting up in your neck of the woods . . . and now I read you've got gypsy moths up there, too?"

"So why not come up and worry with me, Mom? You can help me with the garden, you're so good at that, and the kids would love to have Grandma around all the time."

"I think they like Grandma because she lives in the city. They like to come to visit me in the city. They wouldn't have that chance if I lived with all of you."

"You're just being stubborn."

"Stubborn, yes, but not *just* stubborn. I'm being smart, too. Why should I watch you and your family struggling to better yourself . . . better schools for the kids, nicer furniture, flashier car, when I can sit here in my apartment and look out the window at the Drive and be cozy and at peace with myself and my Maker and watch all you people going home to the suburbs bumper to bumper every night, going home to worry whether the chimney sweep did a good job today or if the new draperies in the living room are long enough?"

"Wow, are you all wound up today!"

"You know how I always like to get wound up when I'm talking to you, Son. I enjoy it."

"So how about moving up here and you could be wound up all the time?"

"You never give up, do you?"

"Just like my mother taught me."

"Aw, go on . . . (City Mom pauses; a cough clears her throat, which might have become a bit choked) . . . give my best to everyone, especially the kids. Give them all a hug from me and . . . and thanks for the call, son."

Yes, God may live in the suburbs, but it seems he spends a lot of time in the city, too.

SUNDAY AFTERNOON
Kicks

For reasons I cannot explain, Sunday afternoon has depressed a great many people. I am not even thinking now about the thousands of Indianapolis Colts fans for whom depression has become a Sunday-afternoon fact of life. I am referring to writers who have put their unhappiness with Sunday onto paper.

Cyril Connolly, for example, noted, "The boredom of Sunday afternoons, which drove De Quincey to opium, also gave birth to surrealism: how propitious for making bombs." How's that for a downer?

And Katharine Butler Hathaway wrote of a Sunday despair that knows no geographic limitations. "Why is Sunday such an empty day, anywhere, city or country?"

Kafka, whom no one would ever have considered calling Sunny Franz anyway, wrote in his diary of "an endlessly dreary Sunday afternoon . . . its every hour a year. By turns walked despairingly down empty streets and lay quietly on the couch. Occasionally astonished by the leaden, meaningless clouds almost uninterruptedly drifting by. 'You are reserved for a great Monday!' Fine, but Sunday will never end."

There's a gloomy outlook for you. But Cyril and Katharine and Franz might have been suffering from what so many suburbanites suffer on Sunday afternoons: they don't know what to do. Stated a little differently, they don't know how to use Sunday afternoons.

There are no more promising hours in the entire week than those between noon and 6 P.M. on a Sunday. For readers, depending on the season of the year, it is a time to stretch out in the sun or to curl up by the fire and catch up on a tome or something shamelessly trivial. For athletes, and those who imagine themselves to be athletes, it's a time to realize dreams and/or fantasies. And for all those people who look for a period of tranquillity to break up those seemingly interminable one hundred and sixty-eight hours of frenzy and tension, Sunday afternoons are (caution: questionable allusion just ahead) heaven.

For B.J., Sunday afternoon, unlike his Monday evenings, is not boring. On the contrary, for B.J. Sunday afternoons are, quite literally, a kick.

The same for his parents. For Janice and Phil, Sunday afternoons, emotionally, are a kick.

In toddlerhood, B.J. never showed any particular athletic prowess. When he was thrown a ball, instead of catching it, B.J. would fall on it. His father would, at first patiently, and later quite testily, show little B.J. how to hold his hands out and away from his body to receive the ball, and when the ball struck his hand to clench his fingers around it.

Every so often B.J. would, in fact, reward his dad with a clean catch. More often, however, B.J. would let the ball bounce off his outstretched hands, and then the boy would fall to the ground and atop the ball, giggling all the while. And Phil? Phil would chuckle despondently. He had hoped B.J. might develop into a headline-making athlete; even a local headline-making athlete would do. But it seemed that the best Phil could possibly hope for was that B.J. would grow up to be a fumble-recovery specialist.

At least that was the best Phil could have hoped for until the Sunday soccer league hit town. All of a sudden, boys and girls who gave no promise of becoming a Dr. K, Dr. J or Martina were running up and down lime-lined fields with all-star abandon. The kids slid, they leapt, they kicked as though they had just discovered a new expression for life —and themselves. Sunday soccer immediately gave hundreds of children the chance to feel good about themselves.

And in this environment, B.J. shone.

B.J. is fast, faster than most boys his age, fast enough to sweep the ball (he is, in fact, the sweeper on the team) and spark the team's offense. His soccer exploits have also sparked a shared parental enthusiasm, a new and keen rooting interest in both the son and the sport. This shared enthusiasm prompts mother and dad to come out every week, spread the old green woolen blanket on the rise overlooking the soccer field, and watch the game.

Shared enthusiasm for anything, after years of marriage, is hard to come by. For example, before B.J. discovered soccer, and his aptitude for it, Janice spent Sunday afternoons at the ballet and Phil spent them in front of some televised football game or other. Now Baryshnikov and Jim McMahon have been replaced by a fast little soccer player who, although he does not have balletic grace, has the brashness to wear a headband.

During a lull in an especially exciting game Phil says, "You know what I like about this whole scene, Janice?"

"What?"

"The people coming up to us and saying what a terrific athlete B.J. is and how we must be proud of him and things like that."

"You really like to hear all that stuff?"

"Yeah, I do. Why not?"

"I don't know why not. I like it too."

And they share a laugh, recalling when they shared just about everything, every minute of the day. Phil's chest may swell with pride when a spectator congratulates him on being B.J.'s begetter, but his voice swells with rage when he sees his son called for an infraction.

"Whattya mean 'offside'? How could that be offside? How could you see it from back there? Say, is this your first soccer game, ref?"

There's a smattering of applause in support of Phil's spleen. He acknowledges the support with a wave as Janice pulls his hand down, as well as his body, to the blanket.

"Take it easy, Phil. Don't make a spectacle of yourself."

"What spectacle? The ref's the one making a spectacle of himself. No way that was offside."

"Phil, a few months ago you didn't know what offside in soccer even meant."

Phil has to smile. It's a sheepish grin, because what Janice has said is true. "Ssssh . . . *they* don't know that." Phil hugs his wife and says to God:

> They don't know much about me,
> At least I hope they don't.
> They don't know about

My insecurity, which I cover up
  With bravado;
My shyness, which I cover up
  With jokes;
My fears, which I cover up
  With faith.

Since I've managed pretty well so far, God,
During whatever lifetime is left me,
Let's keep all of these cover-ups, please,
Just between You and me.
Amen.

Mothers and fathers, even spectators with no apparent relative root-ing interest, rise to their feet as the 1-1 game winds down. With just a minute to play, B.J. intercepts a pass at mid-field and dribbles down the sideline between two defenders. As he is about to be forced out of bounds, B.J. chips a rainbow-arced pass to a teammate rushing toward the goal. The teammate jumps straight up so that his head, making contact with the ball, redirects the black-and-white sphere just out of the goaltender's reach and into the far corner of the net.

The celebration on the field is only slightly more manic than the one on the sidelines. Parents and friends do not pile on top of each other, as do the players. But there is, among the adults, backslapping, jumping, high fiving and a flailing of the arms that is refreshingly adolescent.

What a game! What a life! What a kick!

B.J., sucking on a postgame victory orange, asks, "Where's the car?" He had been picked up an hour before game time by the coach.

"It was a nice day," says B.J.'s mother, "so we decided to walk up here."

"You mean we have to walk home?"

"It's almost all downhill."

Phil adds, "And besides, you're two feet off the ground anyway."

The son smiles and looks up at his father. "Yea, Dad, it must have been exciting to watch, too, huh?"

"You certainly were, B.J., you certainly were."

The walk home, just over a mile, is another renewed shared enthusi-asm. It conjures up memories for Janice and Phil of pushing strollers, carrying children on shoulders, seeing who could walk faster, making sure you didn't step on a crack. Now the walk home is yet another kick, the three of them, the boy in soccer shorts, the man in corduroy and a sweater, the woman in a purple sweatsuit, kicking through the leaves that have been piled up on the street in front of the recently raked lawns.

Phil picks up a handful of leaves and, throwing them at Janice, he shouts, "Quick, what song does this remind you of?

Brushing the leaves out of her hair and off her sweatshirt, Janice yells, "Are you out of your mind?"

"No, that's not it. It's 'Love Me or Leaf Me.' "

Both mother and son groan at yet another atrocious pun from husband and dad. Janice, picking up an armful of leaves, tells B.J. to do the same. "C'mon, B.J., let's get him . . . let's give it to him!" They run down the street in pursuit of Phil, who, after a few paces, gives up and surrenders to a shower of leaves.

What a life! What a kick!

Turning a corner less than a half mile from home, B.J. spots a flashing light in the distance. "Somebody got busted."

"I wish you wouldn't say 'busted,' B.J. Being stopped for speeding isn't exactly 'being busted.' "

"I don't think that's a police car, Janice," says Phil, "I think it's an ambulance."

As the trio moves closer, they see that Phil is right; it *is* an ambulance, and someone on a stretcher is being placed into it. "Isn't that the Eggleston house? Doesn't Bill Eggleston have a heart condition?" Phil hurries on ahead to see what has happened.

As the red/blue light whirls around atop the ambulance, B.J. says to his mother, "Those lights are cool, aren't they?"

"The ambulance light?"

"Yeah, imagine a disco full of them."

"Where did you hear of that?"

"Jen told me."

"Jennifer's gone to a disco . . . full of ambulance lights? She never told me that she . . ."

"No, Mom, no, she saw it in some magazine."

Phil returns to Janice and B.J. with some information. "It's not Bill Eggleston. It's some jogger."

"Oh, my God," gasps Janice. "Hit by a car?"

"No, heart attack, I'm afraid."

"How is he . . . is it a man or a woman?"

"A man . . . and he's . . . dead."

"Oh, no."

"Yeah."

"Do they know who it is?"

"No ID on him and the ambulance crew don't recognize him."

"Oh, dear."

"Funny, isn't it?" says B.J. who, for the past few moments has been uncharacteristically quiet, "you think jogging will make you live longer, and what does it do—kill you."

The remainder of the walk home is in silence. The leaf-kicking, leaf-throwing romp, shattered by a sudden death, has turned mother, father and son quiet. It's a communicative quiet, however, as each turns to God looking for an explanation, some why, how come, what for.

That communicative quiet continues, for a time, at home. Eventually it is broken by a shout from the patio: "How many sweet and how many hot?" Phil, now that the charcoal is ash gray, is ready to put the sausages on. "How many sweet and how many hot?" is one of those warm, woolly phrases that, paradoxically, prompt a shiver of security, a tingle of sublime gladness up and down the backs of family members. That particular line, for Janice and Phil and their children, translates into "We're together," "We're home", "Everything's all right."

These lines, these echoes, differ, of course, from family to family, from raised ranch to colonial manse to mock Tudor town house. The phrases need not be food-related, although many are. "Let's call for Chinese tonight" is one of the most comforting lines spoken regularly in suburb *or* city.

Sentences—declarative, interrogative and even some provocatively imperative—as:

"Who's showering first?"

"Is tonight casual or dressie-Bessie?"

"Collect call from Junior. Will you accept?"

"Tell the oil-of-wintergreen story, Mom."

"Our music going out; *your* music coming back." suggest an intimacy born of time-tested togetherness. And then there's that recent addition to the lexicon of familial warmth and comfort "What do you say we rent a movie tonight?"

All these lines—and any number you can think of that are spoken in *your* family—imply that we creatures of God are not meant to be alone. We rejoice, though the decibel levels of our joyfulness may vary *(our* music going out is always softer than *their* music coming back) in our togetherness.

It's a good life, this suburban existence. As family and neighborhood and community, we share our delights and dilemmas. And it's so reassuring to sense that He does too.